STRUGGLE
AND HOPE

*The Story of
Chinese Canadians*

STRUGGLE AND HOPE

The Story of Chinese Canadians

Paul Yee

UMBRELLA PRESS
56 Rivercourt Boulevard
Toronto, Ontario
M4J 3A4

Dedication

**Dedicated to Adam, Eric, Noah and Ryan,
children who bring joy wherever they go.**

Publisher: Kenneth H Pearson

Editor: Jocelyn Smyth

Cover: Ron & Ron Design & Photography

Cover Photograph: Dan Lim Photography

Cover Subjects: Patrick Dang and Lorraine Leung

Maps: Ron & Ron Design & Photography

The Publisher acknowledges the assistance of the Multicultural Programs of the Department of Canadian Heritage.

Canadian Cataloguing in Publication Data

Yee, Paul
Struggle and Hope: The Story of Chinese Canadians
(Peoples of Canada)
Includes bibliographical references and index.
ISBN 1-895642-14-0
1. Chinese - Canada - History - Juvenile Literature
2. Chinese Canadians - History - Juvenile Literature. * I. Title. II. Series

FC 106.C5Y4 1996	971'004951	C96-931408-3
F 1035. CY 4 1996		

A *kennyp* Publication

Manufactured in Canada

Publisher

UMBRELLA PRESS
56 Rivercourt Boulevard
Toronto, Ontario
M4J 3A4
Telephone: 416-696-6665
Fax: 416-696-9189

Contents

Preface

Over the years, many terms have been used to refer to the people who are the subject of this book. They include Chinese Canadians, Canadian Chinese, Canadians of Chinese descent, and Canadians of Chinese ancestry. These terms reflect different ways in which people of Chinese origin living in Canada view themselves.

Some feel more Canadian than Chinese, because they were born and grew up here, in families that have been in Canada for generations. Others feel that their physical visibility as Asians and their cultural connections to Asia should be proudly acknowledged. Still others feel that Canadians of _____ descent should be used to describe all Canadians as an indication that we are all equal citizens of this country, no matter how long we have lived here.

Paul Yee
Toronto

Introduction

In this book, the term Chinese Canadian refers to Canadians of Chinese descent no matter which country they came from or how long they have lived in Canada.

Today, people of Chinese descent make their home in all of Canada's big cities and in many of its small towns. Some are from families that have lived in Canada for four or five generations; others arrived only a few years – or even a few months – ago.

The first Chinese immigrants came to Canada in 1858. Since then, there have been several waves of Chinese immigration. Each was distinct and so were the conditions under which the immigrants settled. In the 1990s, the majority of Chinese immigrants are from Hong Kong, but Chinese people have also come from South America, South Africa, the Caribbean, China, Taiwan and Southeast Asian countries, such as Singapore, Malaysia, Vietnam and the Philippines. They speak many languages and many different dialects of Chinese. This book discusses the many different kinds of Chinese who are part of Canada today.

The book has two main sections. The first looks at the Chinese in Canada between 1858 and 1967. The early immigrants worked and survived in the midst of a generally hostile White society. Because of physical and cultural differences, they faced prejudice and even violence, restrictive laws and racist community leaders from all levels of society. Nonetheless, Chinese people settled in every province during this period, though most, by far, lived in British Columbia.

The second section of the book deals primarily with the Chinese who came to Canada after 1967. That year, Canada's immigration laws were changed to reflect a dramatically changing attitude to minorities. The Chinese came in larger numbers, bringing higher skills and expectations. Settlement shifted towards central Canada. Ontario, in particular, was a favoured destination, but Chinatowns flourished in cities across the country. The Chinese-Canadian community became more complex.

To understand Chinese Canadians, this book is one place to start.

Part One
Early Generations (1858-1967)

The early immigrants to Canada in the 19th century and the first half of the 20th century came mainly from the southern province of Guangdong.

Chapter One

From Faraway

Canada and China are separated and linked by the vast expanses of the Pacific Ocean. One way of understanding the connections between the two countries is to think of "push" and "pull" factors. That is, events occurred in China that pushed people to leave their homeland. At the same time, developments in Canada pulled immigrants to its shores.

The Opium Wars and the Founding of Hong Kong

For centuries, the West had purchased large quantities of tea, silk and porcelain from China. But there was little that China wanted to buy in return.

Then, in 1773, Britain began selling opium (grown in India) to China. Consumption of and addiction to this drug increased dramatically, leading the Chinese emperor to proclaim a ban on opium-smoking in 1796. Nonetheless, Britain continued bringing the drug into China because it provided high profits.

In 1839, China seized and destroyed six million dollars worth of British opium in order to stop the drug trade. This action led to the "Opium Wars."

The first Opium War (1839-1842) ended with China's defeat and the Treaty of Nanking. Under this treaty, the island of Hong Kong was ceded by China to England, and five coastal ports were opened for trade. This was the first of the "unequal treaties" that forcibly opened China to the West.

In 1860, nine square kilometres at the tip of the Kowloon peninsula and Stonecutters Island were added to the British colony of Hong Kong. This action followed the "Arrow War" during which British and French troops invaded China and destroyed the Summer Palace in Beijing.

In 1898, the British demanded a further enlargement of Hong Kong. In June of that year, China leased 946.6 square kilometres of "New Territories" to Britain for a period of 99 years. The lease on the New Territories will end in 1997. At that time Britain plans to return Hong Kong to Chinese rule.

Why Did They Leave?

In the middle of the nineteenth century, enormous difficulties gripped all regions of China. The early Chinese in Canada came from the coastal farming areas of the south, where hardships resulted from causes that were both internal and external to China.

Between 1787 and 1850, the population of southern China almost doubled, growing from 16 to 28 million. However, there was no increase in food production to match this growth. Farmland was already in short supply, and plots of land shrank with every additional generation. As rents and taxes climbed higher and higher, tenant farmers could not feed their families.

In 1842, China's defeat in the first Opium War led to more problems. As part of the peace treaty with Britain, five new ports in China were opened to international trade. As a result, trade in the major southern port city of Canton (now known as Guangzhou) declined. At the same time, imports of Western machine-made cloth destroyed the cottage industry in which peasant families produced hand-woven cloth to earn extra income.

As well, there was a breakdown in law and order. Twenty million people died when a revolt known as the Taiping Rebellion swept through the nation between 1850 and 1864. Local uprisings in southern China claimed over a million lives between 1853 and 1868. This ongoing warfare prevented peasants from tending their fields. To make matters worse, roving bandits and pirates attacked and raided villages because there were no government troops to defend them. Finally, floods and droughts created additional food shortages and misery.

Confucianism

For centuries, family, society and state in China were based on the official doctrine of Confucianism. During the Han Dynasty (206 BC -AD 220), the teachings of the philosopher-scholar Confucius became the prime textbooks for training government officials and were used until the first decade of the 20th century. Its rules operated at all levels of society.

The goal of Confucian thinking was to achieve a harmonious society where all people knew their station in life and acted accordingly. Women were to defer to men, the young were to obey the old, inferiors were to acknowledge their superiors, and the ruled were to follow the orders of their ruler.

Age was venerated ("the older the better") because it was viewed to give value and credibility to people, objects and institutions. Elderly people might be physically weak, but they were seen to be at the peak of their wisdom.

Confucianism tended to exalt the glories of the past. For example, stories about children who took especial care of their parents were told and retold over the centuries as lessons of model behaviour.

Confucianism also reinforced the central role that the family played in Chinese society. Children had to respect and fulfil their duties to parents. Ancestor worship was an extension of respecting one's elders. In annual ceremonies, families would gather, light incense and present offerings to honour the generations who had gone on before.

In the face of these disasters, many people from southern China left home to seek jobs and opportunities elsewhere. Those who came to North America were mostly men. They were peasants, hired hands or workers, such as pedlars, labourers or tradespeople, from towns and port cities. Those who owned a bit of land some- times sold it to pay for their steamship tickets. Others borrowed the money they needed, and still others signed agreements to work for labour contractors who paid their fare across the Pacific Ocean and then took part of the wages they earned in repayment.

Chinese immigrants at mealtime aboard ship, late 19th century on their way to North America.

Cultural Baggage: What Did They Bring?

The early Chinese immigrants to Canada came with cultural values that had developed over many centuries.

In China, family was seen as the key to peace and order in society. Family power was expressed through a clan, a network of families sharing a common surname. Clans owned land, collected rents and provided loans. They helped the aged and needy, and maintained schools and bridges. All clan members were urged to contribute to the wealth of the clan so that they could all, rich and poor alike, enjoy the prestige linked to land-holdings, money or scholarly status.

For Chinese society to function smoothly, Confucian principles taught people to accept their class background, to work hard, and to obey higher authorities. Younger people obeyed their elders, women deferred to men, and all citizens followed the orders of the state.

Nonetheless, there were ways to get ahead to improve one's position in life. Government service was one. Over the centuries, the state in China had become highly structured and employed a great many officials throughout the country. The Imperial examinations for entrance to government service were open to every educated Chinese. Education was thus an important key to higher status and was respected by everyone.

Along with their strong attachment to family and their respect for authority and education, immigrating Chinese brought with them free-market business practices. Thanks to a tropical climate, south China enjoyed long growing seasons. Peasants sold cash crops at local markets. In towns there were storekeepers and tradespeople, such as shoemakers, carpenters and coopers. In good economic times, trade between the regions of China was brisk. To start businesses, funds could be borrowed from money-lenders or clans. Capital could also be raised by pooling funds with friends and colleagues.

The Chinese came to the New World prepared to work hard for their families and clans. They came from a country where a business economy had flourished for centuries and where many people had achieved success through education and individual enterprise. As it happened, these beliefs and economic principles were also fundamental to North American society.

Chapter Two

First Arrivals: 1858–1923

The first Chinese who settled in North America came in 1848 for the California Gold Rush. Ten years later, as the boom days in California were over, many of them trekked north to British Columbia where gold had just been discovered along the Fraser River. By 1863, four thousand Chinese were working in the Cariboo gold fields of British Columbia.

Chinese gold miners reworked sites that other miners had abandoned when new finds opened up richer sites. Not only were used claims easier and cheaper to buy, but in California the Chinese had been beaten, robbed and kicked off their claims by White miners. British Columbia witnessed similar violence, and therefore the Chinese sensibly avoided crowded new-strike areas.

Washing for gold on the Fraser River.

The Chinese also met many of the frontier economy's needs. They grew vegetables for sale, cut firewood and ran laundries and restaurants. A thousand Chinese helped build the 607-kilometre Cariboo Wagon Road from Yale to Barkerville. Once it was finished, Chinese teamsters drove horse-teams through the perilous Fraser Canyon. In 1866, five hundred Chinese strung telegraph wires through the new colony.

Not all the Chinese who came to British Columbia went to or stayed in the gold rush areas. In the 1870s, fish canneries were established along the coast. Their owners were constantly troubled by labour shortages because the work was seasonal and because White workers tended to leave for the mines at the first opportunity. Chinese crews soon dominated the industry. In Victoria, Chinese worked as servants and cooks in wealthy households. Chinese coal miners worked in Cumberland, near Nanaimo.

Chinese neighbourhoods emerged in the towns and cities of British Columbia because White people did not want the Chinese living near them. These Chinatowns consisted of general stores, rooming houses and shops, such as barbers and herbalists.

At the centre of a Chinatown were the merchants: import-export traders, labour contractors and land-owners. Their stores were gathering places where people received mail, sent money to China or sat around and chatted. Newcomers or travellers could find shelter there. Larger Chinatowns, such as Victoria's, included tailors, bakeries, jewellers, photographers and theatres.

Worker at fish cannery in British Columbia.

Building the Railway

The construction of the British Columbia section of the Canadian Pacific Railway sparked the next major influx of Chinese. Between 1881 and 1885, seventeen thousand Chinese arrived in Canada, most of them recruited to work on the railway. They received a dollar a day, half the wage paid to Whites. In gangs of thirty they cleared and graded the roadbed and secured the rail ties with gravel.

An estimated fifteen hundred Chinese died during this work. Landslides and careless dynamite blasts killed many. Others died because of inadequate living quarters (especially in winter), poor nutrition and a lack of medical care.

The completion of the railway in 1885 put hundreds of Chinese out of work. Many headed towards the prairies and eastern Canada; others went back to China. But most stayed in British Columbia, particularly in the new city of Vancouver that sprang up at the western end of the railway line. Vancouver became Canada's chief western port, where steamships from Asia docked to unload cargoes of immigrants and goods. Its Chinatown soon overshadowed Victoria's as the heart of Chinese settlement in Canada.

Sing a Song of Gold

Attracted by a succession of gold rushes, men had been coming from south China to North America since 1848. They called their destination "Gold Mountain." After the precious yellow metal dwindled, the Chinese found work on the railway, in canneries, in shingle mills, and in many other industries.

Some immigrants sent home gleaming stories of success, as this song from the Taishan area of South China shows:

Don't marry your daughter to a man of books,
He locks the door and sleeps alone.
Don't marry your daughter to a farming man,
Feet full of manure and hair all dusty.
Match her quickly to a man from Gold Mountain,
When his boat comes in, so will money.

Many of the migrants were men with wives at home in China. These women endured lonely and frustrating periods, often for years and years waiting to be re-united with their husbands. They sang different words to the song.

Don't marry your daughter to a man of books,
He locks the door and sleeps alone.
Don't marry your daughter to a farming man,
Smelling of mud that will snuff her life.
Don't marry your daughter to a Gold Mountain man,
Away from home, he won't remember.
Match her quickly to a businessman
She'll have fish for breakfast and meat for dinner.

Building the Railway

In 1871, when British Columbia joined Confederation, Canada promised the new province that a railway would be built to unite the country from sea to sea.

Chinese and other labourers at Muer's Rock .

Chinese workers' camp at Glacier Park, B.C.

Almost immediately, a motion was introduced in British Columbia's legislative assembly to prevent Chinese from working on government projects. Residents knew that thousands of Chinese workers had built the Central Pacific Railroad through California and Nevada and did not want the same to happen in their province. As years passed without the railway being started, British Columbia threatened to leave Canada.

Finally in 1879, the Canadian government launched construction. A New York engineer named Andrew Onderdonk acquired the contracts to build 620 kilometres of the Canadian Pacific Railway from Port Moody on the Pacific Ocean to Eagle Pass, near Revelstoke. He promised to give preference to hiring White workers, but he also indicated that if he could not find enough of them, he would hire Chinese and Native labourers.

By the end of 1880, Onderdonk faced a labour shortage, and workers had to be imported from China. The Canadian government knew that if the railway were ever to be completed, it would have to be built quickly and cheaply.

Almost all the Chinese workers were men between the ages of eighteen and forty. When they signed up, they were promised $1.00 a day in wages. In contrast, White workers were paid $2.00 to $2.50 a day. In one year (1885), about 7500 of the 9000 men working on Onderdonk's contracts were Chinese. In total, between 1880 and 1885, some 15 000 Chinese worked on the railway.

Winter housing for Chinese railway workers.

The Chinese acquired a sterling reputation as railway workers. They worked steadily, looked after their own cooking, and carried their own belongings. They could break camp, hike 40 kilometres, and set up a new camp in 24 hours. It is estimated that their lower wages saved Onderdonk $3.5 million.

When the railway was completed, the Chinese were left to fend for themselves. There was some starvation. Several thousand went back to China, while others stayed to look for work in Canada.

Grave marker, a symbol of the many Chinese who died. The name of the man's home district and village are etched on the two sides of the marker.

Chinese railway work gang.

Moving East

As the Chinese moved east across the prairies and into central and eastern Canada, their settlement and work patterns changed. In British Columbia, they had settled in all areas of the territory and worked in key industries, such as gold mining, salmon canning and coal mining. They also laboured on frontier projects, such as railway building and land clearing. But in the rest of Canada, the Chinese went primarily to towns and cities, where they ran restaurants and laundries. A growing demand for these services provided an ideal opportunity, since such businesses did not require much start-up capital, new language skills or special training.

In 1891, 8910 Chinese lived in British Columbia and only 219 in the rest of Canada. Twenty years later, the population in British Columbia had more than doubled to 19 568, but the Chinese population in the rest of Canada had grown to over 8000. Major settlements were in Ontario, Alberta and Quebec.

Across the prairies, the Chinese settled in small towns along railway lines and opened wash-houses and cafes. In Alberta, some found

Nurses of daughter of J.A. McDonald family in Montreal in 1867.

A Mother' Story

Lillian Ho Wong was born in Vancouver in 1895. She tells this story about her mother.

My mother was fifteen-years old when she came over. What year? Before 1890, I guess. My father took her to Kamloops where she had her first child. He had a store there, selling woollens. When winter came, it was so cold that my mother stuck the baby's feet in the oven of the stove to keep warm. But the baby died. She had another baby, and covered it with a heavy blanket. It died too.

Then there was a big fire in Kamloops, and everything burned down. My father lost everything in his store so he decided to move to Vancouver.

By then my mother had another baby, but this one died on the way down. So they stopped the wagon and dug a hole and buried the baby by the trail. My mother stuck a piece of wood there to mark the spot. She always said she would go back to visit the grave, but she never did. Altogether my mother had nine children.

Chan Sing and his wife in their restaurant in Portage la Prairie, Manitoba. As a mixed marriage, the couple faced discrimination, *but overcame it and had a happy marriage and successful business.*

work in the mines at Anthracite and Bankhead, on the sugar beet farms near Raymond, and on cattle ranches, where they worked mainly as cooks. These jobs were seasonal, and the workers returned to larger cities, such as Calgary, Edmonton, Lethbridge and Red Deer, for the winter.

Moose Jaw, an important railway city, had Saskatchewan's largest Chinatown. Regina, the provincial capital, did not have a Chinatown because early Chinese settlers agreed to establish their businesses at some distance from one another in order to avoid competing among

themselves. The Chinese in Winnipeg made a similar pact, so a Chinatown did not develop there until 1909.

In Ontario the Chinese from western Canada were joined by others coming north from the United States. Major Chinatowns were found in Toronto, Hamilton and Ottawa. Toronto's Chinatown quickly became Canada's third largest Chinatown.

Almost all the Chinese who went to Quebec settled in Montreal. Chinatown was located near the downtown in a neighbourhood of ware-

The Sino-Japanese War

In 1894, the Korean king appealed to China for help when rebels tried to overthrow him. The rebels were supported by Japan, which dispatched troops to the mainland. On August 1, war was declared between China and Japan.

On September 17, 1894, Japan defeated China's navy in a humiliating battle. On land, Japanese soldiers invaded Korea and then northern China. Forced to seek peace, China surrendered the island of Taiwan to Japan in the spring of 1895 and paid an indemnity of 200 million taels of silver.

After the Opium Wars, China had surrendered to European military power several times, but the 1895 loss was different. This time, China had lost to another Asian country. China's national confidence was shaken. How could such a stunning defeat have happened?

The defeat led to the rise of a reform movement, which argued that China needed to change its system of government and education. But China's Manchu rulers resisted reform, and many of the movement's leaders were forced into exile. They travelled to overseas Chinese communities in Southeast Asia and North America seeking financial support.

One famous reformer, Kang Youwei, came to Canada to raise funds for the reform movement in 1899, 1902 and 1904. He established the first North American branch of his Empire Reform Association in Victoria, British Columbia. By 1904, the twelve Canadian branches of the association counted 7000 members.

houses, factories and rooming houses, where washing and cooking services were needed. By 1912, Montreal's Chinese community numbered a thousand, almost the same as Toronto's. Montreal was the transfer point for Chinese travelling east to the Maritimes by train. It also supplied the eastern settlements with goods and information.

Chinese communities in the Maritimes were tiny. All told, fewer than 600 Chinese lived there in 1921, and so few Chinatowns were established. In Newfoundland, which had not yet joined Canada, Chinese immigrants arrived directly from Hong Kong or Europe, or through the United States.

Chinese labourers and supervisors on road construction near Pennant, Saskatchewan, 1918.

Montreal's Flower

Edith Eaton was born in 1865 to an English father and a Chinese mother. Early in the 1870s, the family moved to Montreal. Edith's mother was one of the first Chinese woman to live there.

At age eighteen, Edith got a job at the Montreal Star newspaper, setting type in the composing room. After that, she became a lawyer's secretary. But Edith was a writer and she published articles and stories about life in Montreal. Often she used the name "Sui Sin Far," which is Chinese for "narcissus flower."

Although Edith looked like a White person, she strongly defended the Chinese in her writing. In 1896, for example, she wrote a powerful article for a Montre-al newspaper defending Chinese immigrants against the allegation that they were all disease-spreading gamblers.

She wrote stories about the problems faced by immigrants to North America. Her writing presented new images of China and the Chinese in America. In 1912, *Mrs. Spring Fragrance,* a collection of 37 of her stories, was published by a Chicago firm.

Around 1890, Edith left Montreal and spent twenty years travelling. She worked as a reporter in Jamaica, as a secretary in San Francisco and as an advertising copywriter in Seattle. She returned to visit Montreal many times and died there in 1914.

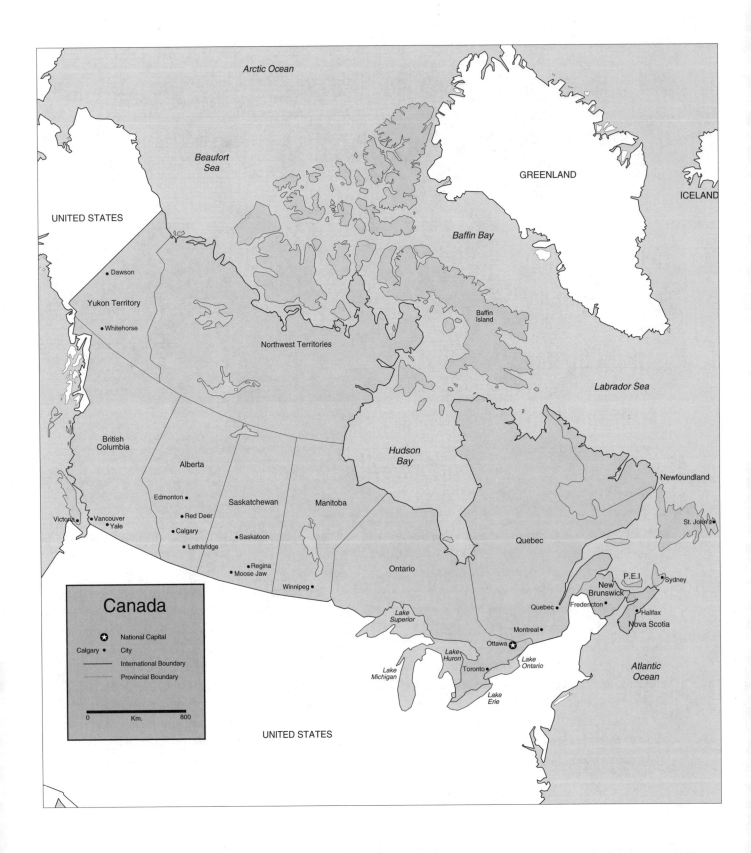

Arctic Ocean

Beaufort
Sea

GREENLAND

ICELAND

UNITED STATES

Baffin Bay

• Dawson

Yukon Territory

Baffin
Island

• Whitehorse

Northwest Territories

Labrador Sea

British
Columbia

Hudson
Bay

Alberta

Newfoundland

Edmonton •

Saskatchewan

Manitoba

Victoria •
• Vancouver
• Yale

• Red Deer

Quebec

St. John's •

• Calgary

• Saskatoon

Ontario

• Lethbridge

• Regina
• Moose Jaw

Winnipeg •

P.E.I.
• Sydney

New
Brunswick

Quebec •
Fredericton •
• Halifax

Montreal •
Nova Scotia

Canada

Lake
Superior

⊛ National Capital

Ottawa ⊛

Calgary • City

Atlantic
Ocean

International Boundary

Lake
Huron

Lake
Ontario

Provincial Boundary

Toronto •

Lake
Michigan

0   Km.   800

Lake
Erie

UNITED STATES

Chapter Three

Anti-Chinese Racism: 1858–1923

From their earliest arrival in Canada, the Chinese had to deal with a fierce racism that was based on two kinds of fear: economic and cultural.

Economic fear focussed on jobs. White Canadians claimed that Chinese workers lived more cheaply than White workers because they ate a lower grade of food, were satisfied with poorer housing and had no families. They could, therefore, it was argued, work for lower wages than Whites could afford to accept and so were hired in preference to White workers. In addition, businessmen accused the Chinese of depressing the economy by sending their earnings to China instead of spending and investing here.

A.D. 1884.

CHAP. 4.

An Act to regulate the Chinese population of British Columbia.

[*18th February, 1884.*]

WHEREAS the incoming of Chinese to British Columbia largely exceeds that of any other class of immigrant, and the population so introduced are fast becoming superior in number to our own race; are not disposed to be governed by our laws; are dissimilar in habits and occupation from our people; evade the payment of taxes justly due to the Government; are governed by pestilential habits; are useless in instances of emergency; habitually desecrate grave yards by the removal of bodies therefrom; and generally the laws governing the whites are found to be inapplicable to Chinese, and such Chinese are inclined to habits subversive of the comfort and well-being of the community: Preamble.

And whereas it is expedient to pass special laws for the Government of Chinese:

Absurd observations about the Chinese were written into laws by governments.

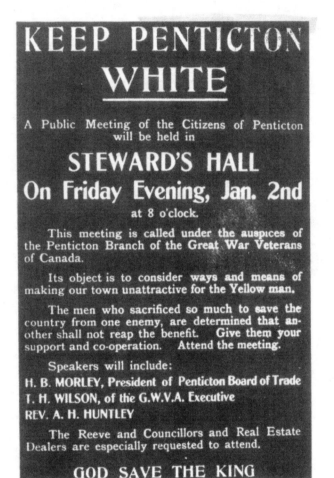

From the Penticton Herald

At the same time, the Chinese were seen as a threat to cultural identity. A White society rooted in European values was attempting to assert itself in North America. It felt that the Chinese could never be assimilated because they were of a different race. They were viewed as dirty and disease-ridden because they lived in crowded conditions. They were looked down upon as morally inferior because of links to gambling, opium-smoking and superstitions.

Anti-Chinese racism took many forms: laws, rock-throwing and other forms of physical assault; taunting of adults and children alike by White youngsters; restrictions on where Chinese could work; and public denunciations by White community leaders. The Chinese were not treated equally when they searched for jobs, housing or services, such as health care. This racism was expressed at all levels of society: by men and women, adults and children, rich and poor, business and labour leaders, politicians and journalists.

Typical home of Vancouver white workingman

A warren on Carrall Street infested by 2000 Chinese

Newspaper illustrations often exaggerated how the Chinese lived.

The Laws of the Land

Anti-Chinese racism was expressed at all three levels of government in Canada – federal, provincial and municipal. In 1885, in order to reduce the number of Chinese coming to Canada, the federal government required that every Chinese immigrant pay a head tax of $50 in order to enter Canada. This tax rose to $100 in 1902 and then to $500 in 1903. Newfoundland, which was not then a part of Canada, passed similar legislation in 1906, with the head tax set at $300.

The province of British Columbia, for its part, passed laws denying Chinese people the right to vote, to own or work on Crown land, or to work on provincial railway projects. Because they could not be entered on the voters' list, Chinese people could not work as accountants, lawyers or pharmacists. Saskatchewan also took the vote away from its Chinese residents in 1908. Over the following decades Ontario, Saskatchewan, Manitoba and British Columbia all passed laws forbidding Chinese businesses from hiring White women. This was based on exaggerated fears that the women might be corrupted.

At the municipal level, Vancouver and Victoria refused to hire Chinese workers. Residents of cities such as Lethbridge, Hamilton and Vancouver complained to City Hall that Chinese laundries lowered the value of their properties, and the cities passed by-laws restricting where the Chinese could set up laundries.

Certificate of head tax paid by Quan Lum, 1912.

A Canadian-born Generation

The first Chinese person to be born in Canada was Won Alexander Cumyow. Born in 1861, he grew up in New Westminster, studied law, and was appointed court interpreter in 1888. His birth marked the start of a small Canadian-born generation of Chinese Canadians.

This generation grew up speaking both English and Chinese, but most of them could not find meaningful jobs here because of racism.

Gordon Cumyow, son of Won Alexander, wanted to become a lawyer. His father introduced him to solicitors willing to article him as a clerk. Gordon worked in their law offices for over two years, but the Law Society would not accept his application. He finally gave up when his employer said, "Cumyow, you're wasting your time; you're not going to get anywhere. You'd better change your profession. If you want to fight them, you've got to have money, you've got to get good lawyers."

Gordon's sister Aylene wanted to become a nurse. "She finished high school and tried again and again to get into nursing school, but they wouldn't take her," recalled Gordon. "My dad tried all the well-known White doctors. No dice. My sisters wanted to get in, too, but they couldn't. After that, they took up stenography. But it was hard to get into an office also because they said, 'We're doing White people's business, why would we hire Chinese?'"

Dick Yip was born in Vancouver in 1907. He said, "It was hard to get a high school education. A lot of people didn't get it because there was a very tough examination called the junior matriculation. Being brought up in Chinatown had its disadvantages because you didn't communicate with any Canadian people, and therefore you didn't speak English properly."

Susan Yipsang was the first Chinese Canadian to enrol at the University of British Columbia. She went on to attend Columbia University in New York, graduating with a Bachelor of Science degree in 1921. After earning a Master's degree in 1922, she went to China to teach. In 1931 she became principal of the Provincial First Girls' School in Guangdong province in China.

By 1923, the Cumyow family had grown to include grandchildren.

Angry Mobs

Many acts of mob violence were directed at the Chinese. In the new city of Vancouver in 1887, a gang of Whites twice tramped through the forest to a site where Chinese land-clearers were working, ripped their camp apart and drove the workers out of town.

In Calgary in 1892, rumours began to circulate that an outbreak of smallpox had originated in a Chinese laundry. Three hundred angry Whites descended on the city's Chinese laundries and destroyed them. The North West Mounted Police had to be summoned to restore order.

A few years later in St. John's, Newfoundland, several boys were tormenting a group of Chinese on the street one night. When the Chinese chased the boys away, one boy twisted his foot and fell. In reaction to allegations that he had been beaten and kicked by a Chinese, a thousand angry men gathered and smashed all the windows of the Chinese laundries.

September of 1907 saw a crowd of 7000 Whites rampage through Vancouver's Chinatown, breaking every single store window. White mobs tried again to invade Chinatown the next day, but police had roped off the area. The Chinese took rocks, bricks and bottles to the tops of their buildings to hurl at the rioters if they came through again.

School Segregation

In Victoria, several attempts were made to separate Chinese-Canadian students from White classmates. In 1901, White parents wanted Chinese students moved into a separate classroom. When the school board ignored their demand, the parents got the support of the Trades and Labour Council and forced the move of the Chinese children.

Six years later, Victoria school trustees ruled that Chinese children could attend school only if they were born in Canada or could understand English. Although the Chinese community protested, partial segregation resulted. Chinese children in grades one to four were placed in a separate school.

In 1921, the school board separated the two hundred Chinese students from their White classmates. This time, the Chinese community protested by withdrawing their children from the segregated school for one year and organizing their own school. The school trustees eventually backed down.

Storefronts in Chinatown were boarded up after the anti-Asian riots in Vancouver , 1907.

Rich Man, Skinny Building

Sam Kee Company's "Skinny Building" is at the far right (arrow). Most of the other buildings in this picture, which was taken in 1944, have been demolished.

When Sam Kee came to testify at the government enquiry into the 1907 anti-Chinese riots in Vancouver, the English-language newspapers were astounded to learn that he owned property worth half a million dollars.

Sam Kee was actually the name of a business firm. Its founder's real name was Chang Toy, but the company and its White customers all called him Sam Kee.

Sam Kee supplied workers for the shingle mills and canneries, handled imported Chinese food, and sold steamship tickets for the Blue Funnel Line. The company also had its own salt herring plants on Vancouver Island, preparing fish for export. It manufactured charcoal and bought and sold wood products such as shingle bolts and firewood. It owned properties that were leased out as stores and hotels. These many lines of business led the company to have extensive dealings with White businessmen.

In 1912, city officials expropriated part of a lot that Sam Kee owned at a busy corner in Chinatown. The city widened the street and left Sam Kee with a narrow sliver of land, thinking that no use could ever be found for it. But Sam Kee put a building on the lot, and it became famous as the narrowest building in the world.

Chapter Four

Community Development: 1911–1947

Despite the prevailing racism, Canada's Chinese community grew as newcomers continued to arrive. After 1911, more women and children began coming, but the majority of immigrants were still men, whose wives and families stayed behind in China. This growth stopped in 1923 when the Canadian government put an end to immigration from China. Nonetheless, Chinese communities continued developing, and they matured throughout the period between 1911 and 1947.

Most of the immigrants who arrived between 1911 and 1923 were young men and boys coming over to join fathers or uncles already here. They attended school for a while and worked, typically as houseboys or helping in a grocery, laundry or restaurant. Once they were acclimatized, some headed to other cities looking for better jobs. After a few years, a young man usually sailed for China to get married. Then he returned to Canada to work, saving money carefully and sending home as much money as he could. In the following years he revisited China whenever possible to see his family and so that he could father children.

With no family and few White friends, those who ran a cafe or a laundry as the only Chinese in a small town could be very lonely. But Chinatowns in larger cities were busy places. There, traditions and ties to China were maintained, and politics, entertainment, family life, sports and battles against racism were organized.

Life was not easy for immigrants working in low-paying jobs. Here a group shares a house in Vancouver in 1902.

The Chinese had formed many organizations based on common surnames (same last name) or common home districts (same geographic county of origin). These associations provided a friendly meeting place as well as many services. They arranged accommodations, helped the needy, and organized the sending of human bones back to China after people had died. Some associations also set up Chinese-language schools and reading rooms.

Fook Toy Wong and family shown outside their restaurant in Elm Creek, Manitoba, 1931. He came to Canada in 1900 with only his friends when he was twelve years old. He worked as a houseboy in Vancouver when he arrived in Canada and later moved to Elm Creek. His wife came to Canada in 1920. They had five children, four daughters and a son, who graduated with his Ph.D. in physics and had a distinguished career with the National Research Council. The family ran the Elm Creek Cafe until the parents retired to Winnipeg.

From Sea to Shining Sea

Lem Wong came to Canada with his uncle in 1897, when he was fourteen years old. They landed in Vancouver and worked together in a laundry. After five months, Lem decided there would be better opportunities away from Chinatown.

With less than $10 in his pocket, he hopped onto a freight train and rode across Canada. His first stop was London, Ontario, where he worked again in a laundry. Then he quickly moved on to Montreal; Springhill, Nova Scotia; and Sydney, on Cape Breton Island.

In each place, he got a job in a laundry. In Sydney, he worked fourteen hours a day and slept in a bed under the counter in the shop. Still, he found time for recreation. He bought a bike for racing and went out and won prize money.

After five years in Sydney, Lem had saved enough to go back to China to get married. Then he returned to Canada and started his own laundry in London. Ten years later, his wife joined him.

In 1915, Lem opened a fancy restaurant, with an orchestra and supper dances. It became famous throughout southwestern Ontario.

Lem's family joined the Presbyterian Church, where they made many friends. He had eight children. Among them there were three doctors, a chemist, a lawyer, a draftsman and a businessman.

Dr. Sun Yat-sen

Dr. Sun Yat-sen has been called the father of the Chinese revolution. In his efforts to destroy the Ching Dynasty through a revolution, he built up much support from Chinese living overseas.

Dr. Sun was himself an emigrant, having left South China in 1878 to live in Hawaii, where he learned the English language. He returned to China and became a medical doctor in 1892. After China's defeat in the Sino-Japanese War, Dr. Sun was convinced that a revolution was needed. He became involved in underground activities, and went into exile in 1895 because the Chinese government would have killed him.

Dr. Sun came to Canada three times. In 1897, he passed through on his way from London to Japan. In London, he had been kidnapped by Chinese consular officials who planned to send him back to China as a prisoner. He escaped, however, and came to Victoria to raise funds and make contacts.

In 1905, Dr. Sun established the Revolutionary Alliance, and by 1910, a branch of the society was formed in British Columbia. In 1910, he came again to Canada to raise funds.

Dr. Sun's third visit in 1911 was the most exciting. He lectured in Vancouver's Chinatown, drawing audiences of over a thousand people each day. His supporters in the Chinese Freemasons (especially in Montreal, Ottawa, Toronto, Victoria and Vancouver) raised over $35,000 for him.

After the October 10 revolution in 1911, Dr. Sun was elected provisional President of the Republic of China. In view of his long history with the overseas Chinese people of Canada, a park in Vancouver was named after him, and a statue of him was erected in Toronto's Riverdale Park.

Dr. Sun Yat-sen was respected across Canada. Here is the site of the memorial service held for him in North Battleford, Saskatchewan.

Ready to Fight

Many Chinese believed that their homeland's growing weakness was at least partly to blame for Canada's racist treatment of them. When China suffered a crushing defeat at the hands of Japan's navy in 1895, urgent calls to reform China's government and military arose. In response, the Chinese in Canada donated funds to support the reformers and revolutionaries who wanted to modernize China.

In 1911, China's monarchy collapsed, and a power struggle that would tear the country apart for decades began. The contending sides had loyal supporters in Canada, where numer-ous newspapers argued their respective cases. Chinese groups in Vancouver, Edmonton, Saskatoon, Lethbridge and Victoria organized military training, and a unit of 200 men went to China in 1915. Later, aviation training was provided near Victoria and in Saskatoon.

During these same years, 300 Chinese Canadians enlisted in the Canadian infantry to fight in the First World War. The Chinese community also supported Canada's war effort by buying government bonds. The Vancouver Chinese community alone purchased over $100 000 in war bonds.

Women and children from an unidentified family of Moose Jaw, Saskatchewan, in early 20th century.

Community Life

In Chinatown, one place where the Chinese might find White friends was the church. The Presbyterian and Methodist churches had set up missions in the early Chinatowns to preach the Gospel, teach English and provide housing for single men. By 1923, about 10 percent of the Chinese in Canada had become Christians. The Christian influence was particularly strong in Toronto. In Montreal, the Roman Catholic Archbishop assisted the Chinese in protesting a provincial tax on laundries. Nuns started a Chinese hospital there in 1918 and one in Vancouver in 1924.

Although Canada's Chinese population remained mostly male, there were about 210 families in Vancouver by 1919, 150 in Victoria and 35 in Toronto. Most cities had at least a few families. The Canadian-born children attended Canadian schools and spoke English. Some even attended university. However, they were not accepted by White society, and had to look for work and opportunities within Chinatown. They worked as translators or in family businesses, and some left for China in hopes of finding work there.

There were many forms of amusement in Chinatown. Opera troupes from China often came through on their North American tours. There were teahouses and restaurants. Gambling flourished, especially among men who had no family here. Since most men could find only low-paying jobs, the chance to win money that might let them return to China or start a small business proved very attractive. Other Canadians also patronized the gamehouses of Chinatown, which were often raided by the police.

Exclusion

In 1923, Canada passed the Chinese Immigration Act that stopped immigration from China for the next twenty-four years. No new arrivals were allowed in. As well, those Chinese living here and wanting to bring their families over could not do so. The Chinese communities in Canada began to shrink.

The exclusion law resulted from the widespread opposition to the Chinese. All kinds of people and organizations, including boards of trade, war veterans' groups, farmers' associations, labour unions, ratepayer groups, elected officials and newspapers, clamoured to shut the door on Chinese immigration.

The 1921 federal election saw the two major parties accuse each other of being sympathetic to the Chinese and Japanese. The economy also made things difficult: in the years after the First World War, a recession caused job layoffs and unemployment.

For a while, there was hope that China might negotiate a treaty with Canada to end the head tax and to control the number of Chinese entries. But no treaty was ever signed because China's government did not control the southern regions where most immigrants came from.

The Chinese communities in Canada organized opposition to the law, but they failed to stop it. When the exclusion act went into effect on July 1, 1923 - Dominion Day, as Canada's national holiday was known at the time – Chinese Canadians called it "Humiliation Day" and refused to have anything to do with Dominion Day celebrations for many years.

Hard Times

The First World War brought prosperity back to Canada after some difficult years. New industries were set up to produce war materials, the demand for Canadian food and forest products increased enormously, and there were jobs for anyone who could work. All this changed quickly after the war. Munitions factories closed, demand for Canadian goods dropped, and returning veterans could not find jobs. By the early 1920s the country was in a recession.

As always in hard times, resentment of Chinese workers increased, especially in British Columbia where most of them lived. In 1923, under pressure from that province's politicians, Parliament passed legislation to stop virtually all Chinese immigration.

The Chinese Exclusion Act, as it became known, shattered the plans of those who wanted, but had not yet managed, to bring their families over. The law came into effect on July 1, 1923. In protest, the enraged Chinese-Canadian community dubbed the day "Humiliation Day" and refused to celebrate the country's national holiday for many years.

With the flow of immigrants cut off, the Chinese population began to shrink. The pioneer generation died or returned to China to retire. Younger men could still go back to China to visit or to marry, but no new immigration was allowed. Between 1926 and 1935, Chinese Canadians made 32 000 visits to China.

Workers at the log slip at the Hastings Sawmill in 1920.

Soccer Champs

On some days during the late twenties and early thirties, Vancouver's Chinatown was almost entirely deserted. Everyone had gone to the park to cheer the community's trophy-winning soccer team.

The Chinese Students' Soccer Club won the Iroquois Cup in 1926, the Wednesday League Cup in 1931, the B.C. Mainland Cup in 1934 and the Spalding Cup in 1937. They also brought home a trophy for sportsmanship.

The Chinese players were slight in build, averaging 59 kilograms. How did they win? Spoon Wong, the goalie, said, "We were faster. They were big but slow. We ran rings around them. We played a kick-and-run game. As soon as we got the ball, we kicked it away and chased it."

"Sometimes we spoke Chinese in games, shouting things like 'Watch him!' or 'Don't let him through!' The other team didn't know what we were saying, so they sent a letter to the club, asking the president to stop us from speaking Chinese."

When the team captured the B.C. Mainland Cup, Chinatown erupted in a wild celebration. A parade with a hired band and honking cars escorted the team back to Chinatown, where a crowd of thousands had gathered. The players held the metre-high cup aloft in an open car as firecrackers exploded all around. Someone pulled a fire alarm, and two fire trucks came clanging. The next day was declared a holiday in Chinatown, with free tea and dim-sum for everyone.

The Depression

The recession of the early 1920s lifted in the mid-twenties, but the good times that followed were short-lived. The stock-market crash of 1929 marked the beginning of the Great Depression, which affected all Canadians but hit the Chinese community particularly hard.

Unemployment was higher in British Columbia than in any other province, and large numbers of Chinese workers were released from the shingle mills. In 1931, 80 percent of the residents of Vancouver's Chinatown were jobless. The traditional clan and home district associations could not help all the needy, and the Chinese had to turn to public relief.

City officials did not want to give the Chinese the same amount of relief as Whites because the Chinese supposedly needed only half as much to live on. The Anglican Church set up a soup kitchen in Vancouver's Chinatown, to which the provincial government gave 16 cents a day per person for food. At the time, needy White people could get meal tickets worth 15 to 25 cents each.

In Alberta, the Chinese received relief payments of $1.12 a week, less than half the amount paid to others. In protest, twenty Chinese men staged two sit-down strikes on the streetcar line. They were arrested on various charges and fined.

An Airplane Built in Chinatown

In 1935, seventeen-year-old Robert Shun Wong read a *Popular Mechanics Illustrated* magazine article that showed how to build a single-seat airplane with a nine-metre wingspan.

Robert, an experienced model airplane builder, was confident he could do it. He started to build the airplane in his family's upstairs apartment in Chinatown. His parents gave him the go-ahead as long as the project didn't interfere with his high school work and Chinese classes in the evening.

The frame was of wood; a used engine was found at an auto wrecker's. The pieces were assembled at an adjacent garage and then at the airport. In July 1937, the "Sky Scout" rolled out onto the tarmac. Robert jumped in and it flew beautifully.

During the Second World War, Robert trained Canadian fighter pilots in Ontario. Later he and his brother started Central Airways, a flying school based at Toronto Island Airport. Over the course of some 35 years, the school trained more than eight thousand pilots, many of whom went on to fly commercial jets. Robert also played a major role in setting training and safety standards for pilots.

Are You An Accomplice In This Crime?

TO THE SHOPPER AND HOUSEWIFE:

Do you know that you are helping to kill innocent men, women and children in China when you purchase goods made in Japan? Now that Christmas is coming—the season of Goodwill upon Earth—do you wish to be a partner in the crimes being committed by the Japanese war-machine? Help us to bring Peace on Earth by taking the bullets out of Japanese guns that are bringing death to the Chinese people!

TO ALL CITIZENS:

When you fail to protest to the Dominion Government against the shipment of nickel, copper, scrap iron and other war materials to Japan you, too, are guilty of murder in the second degree by being a silent partner in the slaughter of innocent Chinese people, who are your good friends and neighbors across the Pacific.

TO THE BUSINESS MAN:

When you buy from Japan or sell to Japan you are helping to destroy Canada's finest market and your own business future. A free and democratic China will buy Canadian products. Japan, if victorious, will close the OPEN DOOR and drive the white business man from Asiatic markets!

HUMANITY AND YOUR OWN BUSINESS INTERESTS DEMAND
COMPLETE BOYCOTT OF ALL GOODS MADE IN JAPAN!

Issued by
THE MEDICAL AID FOR CHINA COMMITTEE

Provincial Office: 615 WEST HASTINGS STREET, VANCOUVER, B. C.

Roy Wrigley Printing & Publishing Co. Ltd.

A Long War

News from China was bad too. When Japan invaded northern China in 1931, 3000 Chinese attended a mass meeting in Vancouver and launched a boycott of Japanese products. During the following months, in spite of the bad economic times, $16 000 was raised in war aid. Full war did not break out until 1937, when the Nationalists and Communists, the two main groups struggling for power in China, formed a united front to fight Japan.

All the Chinese communities across Canada swung into intense fundraising drives that lasted until Japan's defeat in 1945. Money was raised to buy airplanes and ambulances, medical supplies and winter clothing for soldiers and to provide help to refugees and war orphans.

Cities large and small launched enthusiastic campaigns. Women's groups held teas, bazaars and tag days on the streets. Chinese language schools organized contests, parades and theatre performances. In many Chinatowns, every adult male was required to purchase a minimum amount of Chinese war bonds. Those who did not were identified in local newspapers.

During the war years, Canada's Chinese communities collected about $5 million for China's war effort. Montreal raised $400 000, while Winnipeg's Chinatown of 700 people donated $130 000.

During the Second World War, Chinese Canadians were sent overseas for combat.

Changes for the Better

China and Canada became wartime allies in 1941 when Canada, along with the United States and Britain and many other countries, declared war on Japan. In Canada this signalled the beginning of a change in the relationship between White and Chinese Canadians. In Ontario, Chinese fundraisers joined with other Canadians to create the China War Relief Fund. Between 1941 and 1946, this fund raised over $4 million, mostly from the non-Chinese Canadians across the country. During the war, Canada and China upgraded diplomatic relations, and Canada's first ambassador to China was appointed in 1943.

Initially, Canada did not draft Chinese-Canadians into the armed forces. British Columbia politicians worried that the Chinese would claim the right to vote if they fought for Canada. However, Chinese-Canadian volunteers joined the services on their own, and others left Canada to enlist in the American armed forces.

Finally, by the summer of 1944, the need for soldiers had become acute. White war workers complained about being drafted while Chinese were not, and the government extended the draft to Chinese Canadians, who then went into basic training with other Canadians. Chinese worked in shipyards and factories, served as air raid wardens and joined ambulance corps.

The entire Chinese community was determined to demonstrate its loyalty to Canada by supporting the war effort. In addition to funds sent to China, Chinese Canadians purchased $10 million in Canadian Victory Bonds. In 1941, Vancouver's Chinese raised $500 000 with one in every four Chinese subscribing. British Columbia's average was one person in six, while the Canadian average was one in eight.

Secret Agents

During the Second World War, some Chinese Canadians became secret agents serving in a British organization called the Special Operations Executive (SOE). Because they spoke Chinese and could blend in with Asian populations, they served mainly in South East Asia. There, they worked behind enemy lines supporting the local underground resistance movements.

In 1945, Roger Cheng, Jimmy Shiu, Norman Lowe, Ray Chan, and Lewis King were dropped into Sarawak, in northern Borneo. They joined a small British team gathering intelligence on the Japanese prison camps where 2500 British prisoners of war were held.

Ten Chinese-Canadian sergeants were sent into Malaya to help the local resistance disrupt Japanese communication and supply lines, ambush troops and collect information.

Nineteen-year-old Henry Fung of Vancouver was one of several Chinese Canadians who parachuted into the area around Kuala Lumpur, the capital of Malaysia. He worked with an SOE team in sabotaging Japanese communications and harassing their road convoys.

Ernie Louie parachuted into Malaya with another team. The men trekked for six days through 120 kilometres of jungle to find out about Japanese movements and to instruct and supply local guerrillas.

In 1945, Chinese Canadians who had fought for Canada in either World War were given the right to vote before the rest of their community received it.

Many organizations, such as the Chinese Women's Association, provided financial and spiritual support throughout the war.

Victory parade in Chinatown celebrating the end of the Second World War in Vancouver, August, 1945.

White attitudes towards Chinese Canadians improved during the war as newspapers eagerly described Canada and China as wartime allies and praised Chinese-Canadian support for Canada's war effort. After the war, as the horror of the Nazi extermination camps was revealed during war crime trials, racial discrimination became unacceptable. Canada signed the United Nations charter, which contained human rights provisions. As well, the booming economy in postwar years provided jobs and higher incomes for all Canadians.

As a result of these changes in attitude and circumstances, the anti-Chinese immigration law of 1923 was repealed in 1947. In that same year, British Columbia amended its election law, finally granting the right to vote to its Chinese citizens. The right to vote in federal elections followed automatically.

Won Alexander Cumyow casts a ballot in 1949. When the government of British Colombia allowed the Chinese to vote in 1947, this qualified them to vote in federal elections too.

Chapter Five

Transitions: 1947–1967

The world, and Canada with it, changed enormously between 1947 and 1967. So did the Chinese-Canadian community, partly as a result of the broader changes, partly as a result of its own internal dynamics. Immigration resumed, but the buildings and homes in some Chinatowns were destroyed. There was new acceptance on the part of the White majority, and a new generation of Canadian-born Chinese grew up.

Changes in Canada and China

With the repeal of the 1923 immigration law, the shrinking Chinese-Canadian population began to revitalize itself. Between 1947 and 1962, over 24 000 Chinese came to Canada. These numbers were important to a community that had shrunk from 46 519 people in 1931 to 32 528 twenty years later. Increasingly over the period, these newcomers settled in Ontario, Quebec, and Alberta, rather than in British Columbia.

There were still restrictions on Chinese immigration, however. Only the wives and children of Chinese who had become Canadian citizens were allowed to enter Canada. Yet at this time, Canada was accepting thousands of European refugees and immigrants who had no family ties in Canada. Clearly, Canada still preferred new immigrants who were White. The anti-Chinese restrictions were not changed until 1957, and then only after continual protest from the Chinese community.

Events in China also had a major impact on the Chinese-Canadian community. Once Japan had been defeated, the Communists and Nationalists resumed their power struggle. In 1949, the Communists defeated the Nationalist armies and took control of the nation. At that time, North America was gripped by a "Red Scare," the fear that a world-wide Communist takeover would undermine democracy and freedom every-

Civil War in China

When Japan's surrender ended the Second World War in 1945, China was a divided country. The Chinese Nationalists, led by Chiang Kaishek, controlled the south-western provinces. The Chinese Communists, led by Mao Zedong, occupied much of the nation's remaining territory. The United States tried to negotiate a peace between the two sides but failed. Civil war erupted.

At first, the superior forces of the Nationalists made impressive gains as they marched through northern China. However, the armies were soon too thinly stretched over a large territory. The Communists fought with a guerilla strategy, attacking isolated enemy forces and avoiding prolonged battles for cities.

In 1948, three decisive battles were fought. The Nationalists were defeated as thousands of their troops deserted to join the Communists. Chiang Kaishek fled to the island of Taiwan with two million supporters. The United States put a naval blockade around the island to prevent a Communist attack.

On October 1, 1949, Mao Zedong announced the birth of the People's Republic of China in Beijing. Shortly thereafter, Chiang Kaishek proclaimed Taipei to be the capital of the rival Republic of China. With American backing, the Republic of China was given a seat at the United Nations. It was not until 1970 that the Canadian government officially recognized the People's Republic of China.

where. In the United States, "witch-hunts" to weed out Communists in the government and the entertainment industry were underway led by Senator McCarthy. Some Chinese Canadians worried about being linked to an enemy power, while others worried about relatives suffering under Communist rule. They hoped that changes in Canadian immigration laws might help family members escape.

She Joins Husband after Twenty Years

(Story told by Gim-may Wong)

"I was fifteen years old when I was married in 1930. Yuen had gone to Canada as a boy of eleven. Later he came home and was married to a woman, but she died. So then I became his wife. I couldn't go to Canada with him, so I took care of the land in the village.

"Yuen sent money home all the time. We had several fields. I did the work and hired helpers. Yuen came home to see me, but I didn't give birth to children. He wasn't at home, so I adopted a boy. That way, we had a son. He was the only company I had, all that time living in his village away from my family.

"When the Communists came, Yuen sent for us. We went to Hong Kong and stayed with my brother and his family. We bought clothes there and then we flew to Canada. On the airplane, I sat beside a woman also going to meet her husband. She went to Glace Bay [Nova Scotia] and I often wonder what happened to her.

"We landed in Vancouver where I had another brother. We met relatives, went to the park, and took pictures. And then we got on another airplane and went to Regina. Yuen met us and took us to a little town. He had a cafe there. He spoke English, but I didn't. He taught me how to work in the kitchen. We only cooked Western foods: steak, hamburger, stew. I made jelly rolls. There were two waitresses, White girls, who helped in the front.

"The people in town were good, but I was shy. There were no women to talk with. Then a son was born in 1952. Yuen took him to church and baptized him. I was forty years old when I had another son".

Gim-May Wong with her husband Yuen and a friend in Naicam, Saskatchewan, 1952.

Increased Acceptance

In this climate, Chinese Canadians found greater tolerance from their fellow citizens. However, this acceptance was not complete, so many Chinese, especially those born in Canada, strove to prove they were true Canadians. Some took care to distance themselves from Communist China, insisting that they were Canadians first.

Because those born in Canada spoke English fluently, they were able to work outside Chinatown, and many moved to White neighbourhoods. They formed clubs not linked to traditional Chinese organizations. In Victoria, Vancouver, Toronto, and Montreal, professionals started chapters of the Lions Club International. After the outbreak of the Korean Conflict in 1950, war veterans in those same cities as well as in Calgary, raised money for a "Chinese Community Canadian Troop Comfort Fund" to show their solidarity with Canada's war effort.

The most dramatic changes occurred in British Columbia, where Chinese Canadians had been shut out of professions for many years. The 1950s witnessed a flurry of "firsts" as they now became notary publics, medical students, pharmacists, lawyers and accountants. In 1957, Douglas Jung was elected to Parliament to represent the riding of Vancouver Centre.

Douglas Jung. As a Member of Parliament, Douglas Jung represented the riding of Vancouver Centre from 1957 to 1962. He was the first Chinese Canadian to be elected to Parliament and also represented Canada at the United Nations.

Jean Lumb was the only woman in the Chinese-Canadian delegation that went to Ottawa to meet the newly elected prime minister, John Diefenbaker, in 1957. For ten years, Canada's Chinese community had been protesting the restrictive immigration laws that prevented Chinese families from being reunited. The delegation wanted fairer treatment for Chinese Canadians.

Jean was born in Nanaimo, British Columbia, but moved to Toronto in 1935 as a teenager. She started a fruit store and later operated a restaurant. She served as president of the Chinese Women's Association of Ontario.

In the 1960s, Jean headed the Save Chinatown Committee in Toronto when plans to build a new City Hall threatened to completely destroy old Chinatown. Over forty Chinese organizations protested to the government officials, and the result was a civic designation for Chinatown.

In 1976, Jean was the first Chinese-Canadian woman named to the Order of Canada. A year later, she received the Queen's Jubilee Medal.

New Generations

But these moves towards assimilation were limited for the community as a whole because there remained many who lacked English language and western social skills. Immigrant teenagers who had grown up in China or Hong Kong now struggled to learn English, to adjust to fathers they had seldom or perhaps never seen, to adapt to a new homeland and to find work. In Chinatown, these young people formed basketball teams, orchestras and other new clubs that reflected a younger generation's interest in sports, arts and politics.

At the same time, the arrival of wives from China introduced another group of non-English-speaking Chinese. For the women who came from the villages of South China, coming to Canada meant adjusting to husbands from whom they had been cut off, modern appliances, and even factory workplaces. Reunited couples, along with existing local families, produced another generation of Canadian-born Chinese. This generation grew up in tolerant and prosperous times, eagerly absorbed North American culture through television, attended public schools and went on to university.

In the 1960s, members of the Chinese community, new immigrants as well as pioneer immigrants and those born in Canada, faced a common concern: the demolition of their Chinatowns. Many buildings and businesses had been deteriorating as people moved away. Chinatowns were

Jean Lumb is sitting to the left of Prime Minister John Diefenbaker, Dock Yip is standing behind the Prime Minister and Roland Michener, who would later become the Governor General of Canada, is fifth from the right.

in danger of becoming run-down slums that the Chinese no longer seemed to need.

Municipal governments in Vancouver, Edmonton, Calgary, Winnipeg, Toronto and Montreal made plans to redevelop their downtown areas. The plans proposed replacing Chinatowns with new civic buildings, public housing projects or freeways. Though many Chinese had moved away, many remained – and remained deeply attached to the corner of the city that was home to them. In Vancouver, Edmonton and Calgary, Chinese Canadians challenged city planners and succeeded in stopping the destruction of these historic neighbourhoods.

George Mark, Winnie, his wife, and their two children shown at Gilbert Plains, Manitoba, 1955. George Mark was born in China in 1908 and came to Canada in 1922 to join his father, Sing Mark, who operated a laundry, and later a restaurant in Russell, Manitoba. In 1926, George returned to China to marry and stayed two years before returning to Canada. He made several visits back to China before his wife and children could join him permanently in Canada in 1955. He owned a restaurant in Gilbert Plains, Manitoba, and worked until his retirement. George died in 1976. Both children graduated from university and the son, Inky, became a teacher and later the mayor of Dauphin, Manitoba.

Atta Chong Laundry has been providing laundry service in the east end of Toronto since 1921. In 1913, Sear Foo Lew came to Canada at the age of 18 and worked at various jobs. He returned to China from time to time and in 1937 his son, Chak Fee Lew was born there. Even though he had come to Canada in 1913, it wasn't until 1949 that his wife and son, Chak Fee Lew, were able to join him in Canada. Finally, in 1954, father and son bought the Atta Chong Laundry from the original owner and it is still operated by Chak Fee Lew, shown outside the store.

Part Two
Recent Times (1967 – Present)

After 1967, the Chinese community in Canada grew dramatically as more and more immigrants arrived from around the world. This growth reflected international conditions as well as internal developments. Canada's birth rate had dropped, and the government saw immigration as one way of maintaining population levels, encouraging economic growth and supporting the social security system.

Chapter Six
A New Community: Background 1967–1991

Growing Population

Before 1923, the majority of Chinese immigrants came directly from China. Most were peasants who had little education and were unable to speak English. Those who arrived after 1967 came from many places, including China, Hong Kong, Malaysia, Singapore, the Philippines, southern Africa, Latin America and the Caribbean. Many came from busy urban centres, and some of these immigrants were well educated and English-speaking.

Some came to Canada because of the instability and unrest in their various homelands. Canada, they felt, offered a better way of life, with stable democratic institutions and guaranteed freedoms. Many who came from densely populated cities in Asia wanted to live somewhere with less crowding and less pollution.

The most visible aspect of the growth in Canada's Chinese community was the renewal of old Chinatowns and the emergence of thriving commercial centres. In Vancouver, Calgary and Winnipeg, decaying downtown Chinatowns were revived as storefronts were renovated and gleaming new buildings erected. In suburbs of other major centres, such as Scarborough in Metropolitan Toronto, new shopping plazas with Chinese restaurants, stores and offices emerged. In smaller cities, Chinese businesses replaced older shops on one or two blocks to provide convenient shopping and gathering areas.

This growing community had many consumer needs. People went to Chinese supermarkets, bookstores and fashion shops. They needed familiar foods and dined at specialty restaurants. Chinese-speaking doctors, lawyers and accountants provided essential services. People rented video-tapes and bought music and entertainment magazines imported from Asia. They visited settlement agencies for information and attended language and citizenship classes. International editions of several Chinese newspapers became available.

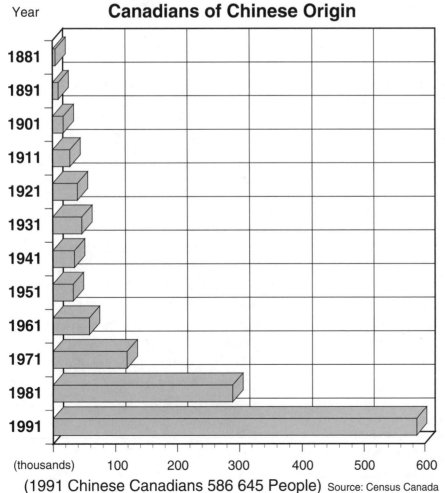

Year — **Canadians of Chinese Origin**

1881
1891
1901
1911
1921
1931
1941
1951
1961
1971
1981
1991

(thousands) 100 200 300 400 500 600

(1991 Chinese Canadians 586 645 People) Source: Census Canada

Immigration Law

Since 1967, three aspects of Canada's immigration policy encouraged the growth of the Chinese community.

- In 1967, Canada started admitting immigrants on the basis of a "point system" that allowed it to select people who were educated and skilled. An "independent" applicant received points for his or her level of education, ability to speak English or French, work experience and other factors, and Chinese applicants were treated in the same way as anyone else. As a result, many Chinese immigrants who were fluent in English and trained in a profession or trade were able to come in through the "Independent" class.

- Canada continued its policy of reuniting families, and so immigrants who became landed residents could apply to bring over members of their immediate family. Chinese immigrants who came as sponsored relatives were less likely than their independent counterparts to speak English or have educational qualifications. Many tended, therefore, to work in lower-paying jobs in the garment or service industries.

- About the mid-1970s, Canada began making efforts to attract foreign business immigrants who could bring in capital and entrepreneurial skills to help the Canadian economy. These efforts were particularly successful with Hong Kong Chinese who were beginning to worry about their future.

The combined admissions of independent and family-class immigrants resulted in the steady growth of Canada's Chinese population. Between 1961 and 1965, 11 785 Chinese immigrants had come into the country. Between 1966 and 1970 that number almost tripled to 33 618, and then it jumped to 56 713 between 1971 and 1975. Hong Kong alone lost 67 000 of its people to Canada in the period 1972-1978 and 130 410 between 1988 and 1992. Direct investment from Hong Kong grew from $10 million in 1967 to $426 million in 1986 and to $2.3 billion in 1991.

In 1994, the federal government announced major changes to the national immigration policy. In the future, it would reduce the number of family-class immigrants (sponsored relatives) and increase the proportion of independents (including business immigrants). This may affect the inflow of Chinese people to Canada.

Canadian Charter of Rights and Freedoms, 1982

Clause 15 (1): Every individual is equal before and under the law and has the right to the equal protection and equal benefit of law without discrimination and, in particular, without discrimination based on race, national or ethnic origin, colour, religion, sex, age or mental or physical disability.

Equality

One reason immigrants were attracted to Canada was the existence of laws that gave them full and equal rights as citizens. However, racism was still alive in Canadian society, and various government measures were undertaken to ensure fair treatment of Chinese and other minorities.

Starting in 1961, federal, provincial and territorial governments passed human rights laws to prevent discrimination. An official national policy of multiculturalism was introduced in 1971 with the express aim of developing the multicultural heritage of Canadians while working to achieve equality for everyone in all aspects of life. As well, many cities created race relations committees and devised policies to deal with racial issues. Governments also funded settlement services and language training for immigrants.

All these measures try to create an environment in which all immigrants and racial minorities can live and work together as equals. But not all Chinese Canadians feel that full equality has been achieved.

Some feel that there are still barriers in hiring and promotion practices at the workplace. They do not find adequate representation of Asian Canadians in the mainstream mass media. Others feel that racial minorities are unfairly linked by sensational media accounts to social problems such as organized crime.

The Canadian Multiculturalism Act, 1988

This Act was introduced in the House of Commons on December 1, 1987. After a series of public hearings, it was approved by Parliament on July 12, 1988, with no dissenting votes, and was approved by the Senate on July 21, 1988. Among its provisions, the Act provides the following:

3 (1) (e) Underlines the commitment made in other sections of the Canadian Charter of Rights and Freedoms (sections 15 and 27) to promote equality for all and to create the social conditions that would further the goal of equality.

3 (1) (g) Recognizes that the social, economic and cultural life of the country is strengthened by bringing together Canadians of different backgrounds.

3 (1) (h) Recognizes that the expression of Canada's multicultural heritage contributes to the richness of our cultural experience. Canadian cultural expression evolves from the experience of individual Canadians and their communities. In applying the policy, the government assists Canadians to understand and share the many cultural influences across Canada, and encourages Canadians to participate in a variety of cultural activities.

Inside the Developing Community

The waves of immigration during this period soon transformed the Chinese-Canadian community into a predominantly immigrant world. Some newcomers organized service agencies to help non-English speakers find work, learn English, obtain government services and legal aid, and acquire citizenship. Others, reflecting the

In Toronto's downtown Chinatown, one of several Chinese-Canadian communities in the Metropolitan area, can be found cultural, religious, social and commercial facilities.

In Chinese communities services, such as banking, are provided in English and in languages that are known to the customers.

diversity within the community, formed organizations among themselves (the Chinese from the Philippines, for example) for social, cultural and educational purposes.

Canadian-born Chinese had adapted to Canadian culture, and many felt little or no attachment to a Chinese community and its activities. Others, however, were concerned that their Canadian-born children did not retain any Chinese culture, and so they organized activities such as Chinese language or folk-dance classes for them. Still others argued that Chinese Canadians possessed a unique history in Canada and that this experience should be explored along with cultural references from China. In 1970, Canada finally established diplomatic relations with the People's Republic of China, and many Chinese Canadians were able to visit their ancestral homeland for the first time.

The Chinatowns of Canada remained the focal point of the community, where new and old organizations, as well as newcomers and old-timers, met to address changing issues. Coalitions were often formed with non-Chinese groups to enable coordinated action. In 1969, a national conference was organized in Calgary to see how urban renewal was affecting Chinatowns across the country. Three years later a new society was formed in Vancouver to build a Chinese Cultural Centre, which opened in 1980. In 1975, another national conference was held to protest the federal government's proposal to reduce immigration levels.

In the 1990s, in recognition of the growing numbers of Chinese settled in neighbourhoods far from the downtown historic Chinatowns, social and cultural activities joined the economic services already available in the suburbs. In

The Jade Water Pavilion of the Dr. Sun Yat-sen Classical Chinese Garden located next to the Chinese Cultural Centre in Vancouver. The Centre was founded in 1972 to build a bridge of understanding between Chinese Canadians and the Canadian community at large. The garden opened in 1986.

the Vancouver area, organizations such as the Chinese Cultural Centre and SUCCESS (United Chinese Community Enrichment Services Society) established satellite offices and programs in suburbs. By 1994, SUCCESS had program offices in Vancouver (4 locations), Richmond, Burnaby-Coquitlam, and at the Vancouver International Airport.

In the Greater Toronto Area, plans were made for a cultural centre and a nursing home for Chinese seniors for Scarborough. Chinese Information and Community Services (CICS), a counselling and referral organization with almost thirty years of history, has set up several offices in Scarborough and nearby Markham.

A Prairie Centre

Part of the ceremony at the opening of the Calgary Chinese Cultural Centre in 1992.

In late 1994, it was announced in the Calgary *Herald* newspaper that the largest Chinese shopping mall to be found in Canada would be located in that city, not Toronto or Vancouver.

Local entrepreneur Sam Switzer invested $20 million into converting the corporate offices of a trust company located near the city's historic Chinatown into the "Dragon City Mall". The fifty Chinese businesses would include restaurants, stores and services. There would be two furniture stories, herbal shops, a driver-training school, and a coffee shop serving 55 flavours of coffee.

In 1994, Calgary had a population of 60 000 Chinese Canadians and expected to receive about 2500 Chinese immigrants a year in the future.

In previous years, the Chinese-Canadian community in Calgary had already established a Chinese Cultural Centre and a Cultural Museum. Both institutions were generously supported by volunteers and private donations. An exhibition on a hundred years of Chinese history in Calgary was held, as well as displays of antiques, arts and archaeologicial items from China.

Chapter Seven

A New Community: Homelands

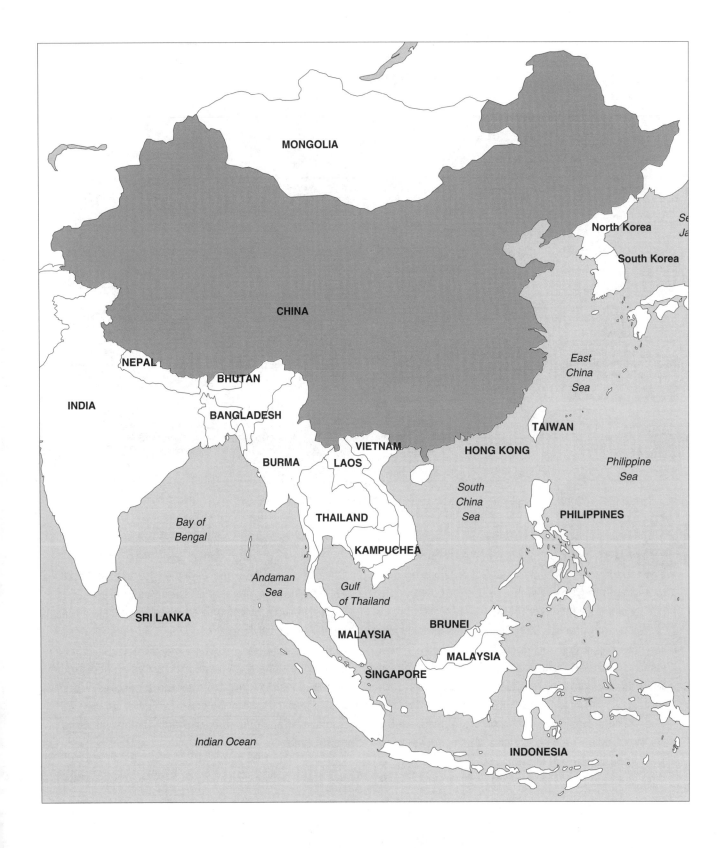

A study of the contemporary Chinese-Canadian community requires a look at different homelands because immigrants reflect both their old and new worlds. Since 1967, Hong Kong and China have been major source countries of immigrants to Canada, but people of Chinese ethnic origin have been coming to Canada from all around the world. These immigrants spoke different languages and hailed from both modern, urban societies and rural, traditional worlds. Among the newcomers have been anxious refugees as well as confident professionals.

Hong Kong Riots of 1967

When the People's Republic of China was established in 1949, it was expected that the Chinese Communists would invade Hong Kong. They had long denounced the "unequal treaties" of the nineteenth century and never formally recognized Britain's control of Hong Kong. However, they made no military advances towards the colony.

In 1966, Chairman Mao Zedong started his "cultural revolution" because he thought China was slipping back towards capitalism. He purged the army and government of his opponents and unleashed the Red Guards, teenagers who viciously attacked authority figures such as teachers, professors, writers and artists.

In 1966, Red Guards invaded Macau, the Portuguese territory across from Hong Kong, and plastered it with posters. Portuguese troops fired on the Red Guards and killed eight of them.

A few months later, violent demonstrations against British rule took place in Hong Kong, inspired by the Red Guards. There were strikes and bombings, and martial law was imposed. The entire economy came to a halt. In July, 300 Chinese soldiers crossed the border and killed five Hong Kong policemen. Property values dropped sharply and so did trade and tourism.

But China needed the foreign currency channelled through Hong Kong's trade activities, and by the end of the year, order was re-established. Nonetheless, the riots made Hong Kong residents worry about a Communist takeover. Many looked for ways to emigrate and Canada soon became a chief destination.

In 1984, China and Britain reached an agreement to transfer Hong Kong back to Chinese rule in 1997. Under the agreement, it will become a "special administrative region" with much control over its government, except for foreign policy and defence. It is intended that Hong Kong retain its capitalist economy within China's socialist system for fifty years after 1997.

Hong Kong

Hong Kong's story is unique. It is a tiny British colony, only 1000 square kilometres in area. It has no natural resources of its own, except for a deep-water harbour and people. With 5.8 million people, it has one of the highest population densities in the world.

Yet Hong Kong ranks among the world's top 12 trading powers. The 140 international banks located in the colony have made it a global financial centre. It is a major exporter of textiles, toys and watches, and although there is a huge gulf between the rich and the poor, overall wages are the second highest in Asia.

Immigrants from Hong Kong are proud of a territory that has achieved such stunning economic success in the years after the Second World War. Hong Kong's lifestyle, based on free enterprise capitalism, has flourished even though the People's Republic of China, a Communist superpower, is its next-door neighbour. Hong Kong possesses an urban, cosmopolitan outlook that is open to influence from Japan, North America and Europe. It has a flourishing entertainment industry with TV and movie stars, pop singers and music videos. Moreover, Chinese culture has survived and evolved freely in Hong Kong, whereas in China many traditions have been destroyed.

Much uncertainty lies ahead, however, because the British are scheduled to return the colony to China in 1997. Members of the educated middle class (teachers, social workers, engineers, accountants and other professionals) have enjoyed high incomes and want to keep their freedom and lifestyle. Fear that this will not be possible under Communism has led many people to leave. For the three years between 1991 and 1993, Hong Kong ranked first among all the source countries of Canada's business immigrants. For 1991, 1992 and 1993, Hong Kong supplied 36, 47 and 42 percent respectively of Canada's business immigrants.

Astronauts

A 1994 report from the Chinese-Canadian Association in Hong Kong estimated there were 80 000 Chinese Canadians working in Hong Kong. One quarter of them had been born in Canada. These business people spent much time flying back and forth between Asia and Canada as they worked.

While many of them considered Canada to be home, Asia's economy was developing rapidly in the 1990s and offered many opportunities to make money. However, the travelling took a toll. One astronaut said, "Sometimes I wake up in the middle of the night and I don't have any idea where I am".

Some travellers gave up the astronaut lifestyle to settle in Canada with their families. Others who were not able to find suitable work here in Canada had no choice but to make the trans-Pacific commute. In a few isolated instances where both parents were working, ten- and twelve-year old children were left alone to take care of themselves in Canada. Even if the mother remained with the children, there still could be difficulties for the family if she could not drive a car or speak English. In these cases, the children often shouldered adult burdens to keep the family going.

A survey by *Ming Pao Daily News* released in 1995 revealed that one quarter of Chinese-Canadian families in the Greater Toronto Area had one member of the immediate family who regularly went abroad to work in Hong Kong, Taiwan or China. However, a clear majority of respondents (64%) said they had never considered returning to their country of origin.

Taiwan

Taiwan, an island located 160 kilometres off the coast of China, is another crowded region of Asia. Like Hong Kong, Taiwan has a highly educated, hard-working labour force working in a modern economy that produces high-tech goods such as computers, television and cameras. But unlike Hong Kong, Taiwan has almost achieved self-sufficiency in food production.

Nonetheless, people are leaving the country. Over 7000 Chinese from Taiwan came to Canada in 1992. The majority (79 percent) of them were business immigrants, reflecting Taiwan's dynamic economy as well as Canada's particular interest in this class of person. For the three years between 1991 and 1993, Taiwan ranked second among all source countries of Canada's business immigrants. For 1991, 1992 and 1993, Taiwan supplied 17, 20 and 21 percent respectively of Canada's business immigrants. The main reason people want to leave Taiwan is that Taiwan, like Hong Kong, is threatened by mainland China, which has never acknowledged the island's right to exist as a separate state.

The freedom and political stability of Canada have proven very attractive to the people of Hong Kong and Taiwan. Some immigrants from these two homelands are nicknamed "astronauts" because they frequently fly long distances between families settled in Canada and business opportunities in Asia. However, immigrants from Hong Kong and Taiwan come from all kinds of backgrounds and include skilled and unskilled workers as well as business people and professionals.

China

The People's Republic of China is the second largest source country of Chinese immigrants to Canada. In the seven years between 1986 and 1992, 44 068 immigrants arrived in Canada from China. This is compared to the largest immigrant source (Hong Kong) with 155 763 immigrants in the same period.

While China is the world's oldest living civilization, it is also a young country where one-third of its people are under the age of fifteen and the economy is a "developing" one.

Since 1949, China has been a Communist country. One political party dominates the government and economic and cultural institutions. Under Communism, the people's standard of living has improved: rural families account for 74 percent of China's population and most of these people now have adequate food and clothing, and great advances in education and health care have occurred.

Starting in 1984, new policies were introduced to speed up modernization. China welcomed foreign investment capital and technical expertise. A free market emerged, allowing peasants to own small plots of land and to grow what they want. In cities, many small stores, restaurants and repair shops are privately owned.

Still, people are leaving China because of better conditions abroad. In China, unemployment and inflation remain problems. As well, massive protests calling for political reform hit twenty cities in 1989. A million people occupied Tiananmen Square, in the centre of China's capital city of Beijing. They wanted a more open society, democracy and an end to government corruption. After two months, army tanks rolled in and soldiers opened fire on the people. As a result, some 800 people were killed. This prompted other Chinese to seek refugee status in Canada.

Nonetheless, with a population of 1.2 billion and an economy that has recently been growing at a rate of 20 percent in some areas, China is viewed as a great economic opportunity for countries like Canada. In 1994, the Canadian prime minister led a delegation of provincial premiers to China and signed agreements worth $8.6 billion. Many Canadian firms are doing work there, and the language abilities, business skills and cultural awareness of Chinese Canadians are increasingly being seen as Canada's "hidden advantage" in the fierce competition for China's market.

Refugees

Many Chinese have come to Canada as refugees. Between 1975 and 1978, Canada accepted 9000 refugees from Vietnam and Cambodia (later Kampuchea). Another 60 000 followed in 1979-1980 from Vietnam, Cambodia and Laos, and it has been estimated that between 70 and 80 percent of those from Vietnam were Chinese.

Chinese, both immigrants and locally born, had lived in these agricultural Southeast Asian nations for many years, chiefly as merchants and traders. They formed 5 percent of Vietnam's population and 6 percent of Cambodia's.

The Vietnam War, which pitted the southern part of the country against the north and the United States against the Communists, ended in April 1975. Subsequently, the Communists were also victorious in neighbouring Cambodia and Laos.

After the war ended, Vietnam faced major hardships. Floods and droughts caused food shortages. Farmlands remained war-damaged from bombs and herbicides. Plans were made to send people from the overcrowded cities to work in underdeveloped regions where they faced rugged conditions, hard work and little

food. In March 1978, the government took over most private businesses, dealing severe losses to the Chinese. When Vietnamese armies invaded Kampuchea in 1978, Vietnam took additional measures against its Chinese (firing them from long-held jobs, for instance, and withholding their ration cards) because China supported Kampuchea.

These factors caused thousands of Chinese and native Vietnamese to flee. Many took to the open seas in unsafe boats, where they fell prey to storms, malnutrition and pirates who robbed them. When boats managed to land on neighbouring shores, they faced an uncertain welcome. Those countries were already burdened with over-crowding and struggling economies. They feared that a large number of refugees would destroy social and political stability.

For example, between 1975 and mid-1979, 167 000 refugees arrived in Malaysia. Of these, 49 000 were towed back to sea, and 42 000 were resettled in other countries. The rest remained in refugee camps.

More than 80 000 Vietnamese fled their homeland in the years after 1976. By 1995, some 46 000 were still left in detention camps scattered throughout southeast Asia. If no third country accepts them, they would be compelled to return to Vietnam.

After settling and establishing themselves in their new homelands, refugees often sponsored other family members to join them. A detailed study of the Canadian integration of the "boat people" refugees between 1981 and 1991 found that, on average, they received less social assistance and unemployment benefits than other Canadians. Their use of health services was about the same as that for all Canadians.

Chapter Eight

The Community Today

Young dancers perform a Chinese "Peacock Dance" at the Spadina Festival in Toronto.

The Chinese-Canadian community has grown from diverse roots. Some of its members were born in Canada, while others are recent immigrants who have come from a variety of homelands. Some speak no Chinese, others speak no English. Many speak one or another of the dialects of Chinese or the languages of their recent homelands. Still, Chinese Canadians are like all other Canadians. They eat, go to work, worry about money and want their children to do well. But they have special concerns about issues that relate to being a racial minority and to being immigrants. Of course, not all Chinese Canadians are immigrants, and therefore not everyone has the same concern over all these issues.

The Toronto Canadian Chinese Youth Orchestra led by Wei Fen Wang, with Ming Xao Sheng and Mizi Tam (shown left to right) at the Toronto Canadian Chinese Artists Centre.

The Issues of Settlement

Immigration is often traumatic because people give up everything that is familiar to them – homes, friends, landscapes, ways of doing things. Upon arrival in a faraway country, they must absorb enormous amounts of new information, including a new language. How fast an immigrant adapts to Canada depends on factors such as age, ability to speak or learn English or French, education level, family status, class background, support of friends and relatives and personal expectations.

A number of immigrant organizations are concerned about access to public social services. Many newcomers do not speak an official language, and few mainstream institutions understand the languages they do speak or the special needs that may be created by their cultural backgrounds. As a result, immigrants cannot get treatment equal to that which other Canadians receive (at hospitals, for example) even though they pay taxes like everyone else.

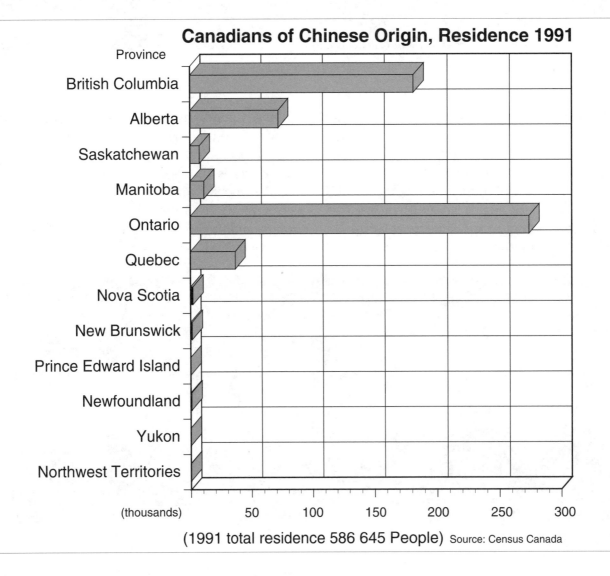

Canadians of Chinese Origin, Residence 1991

(1991 total residence 586 645 People) Source: Census Canada

A related issue involves the trades and professions. Often immigrants with training and years of experience arrive in Canada and find that the tests and courses they need in order to qualify are designed to protect people who trained in Canada. Immigrants looking for work may not find any that matches their qualifications, and so they are often obliged to accept jobs that are lower paying and less satisfying.

Immigrants who lack official language ability may feel doubly disadvantaged as they search for work. Very often, they are told they need Canadian experience to qualify for jobs, yet no one is willing to employ them to provide that experience. They must also make a difficult decision between taking the first available job or taking the time to learn an official language in order to improve their opportunities.

Today, churches, schools and social centres provide support for people in the community.

Backlash in Scarborough

After 1967, many Chinese newcomers settled in Metropolitan Toronto. By 1979, one-third of the region's 150 000 Chinese lived in Scarborough, a suburban community northeast of the downtown. However, the Chinese arrivals were sometimes met with hostility.

In the early 1980s, Glen Watford and Agincourt area residents complained about the increased automobile traffic resulting from the growth of Chinese businesses in local shopping malls. In 1984, a new mall called the Dragon Centre was added to the area with a large restaurant and over 20 stores. This worsened problems with parking and traffic jams. Now residents complained that Chinese people did not fit into the neighbourhood. One woman gave out a pamphlet that called for readers to lobby the federal government to change immigration policy.

In response, the Federation of Chinese Canadians in Scarborough was formed, and Scarborough City Council passed a resolution condemning anti-Chinese hate literature such as the pamphlet.

Two years later, there were plans to build another shopping mall in the area with a 440-seat Chinese theatre, a 130-seat restaurant and other businesses. After local protests, the plan was dropped.

Throughout Scarborough and other Toronto suburbs, however, as well as in other suburbs such as Richmond, near Vancouver, Chinese businesses have continued and flourish.

Cultural Conflict

Immigrant families often encounter problems when parents retain homeland values while their children become "Canadianized." Every family's experience is different.

Most parents expect their children to work hard at school and do well academically. Teenagers struggle to perform well and to please their parents, but some may get little positive feedback. Some parents think that sports are a waste of money, whereas their children find that recreation is a key part of making friends, fitting in and having fun.

Within the family, parents sacrifice a great deal for their children as a way of showing their love.

But some parents might be reserved when it comes to openly showing affection. This can lead to misunderstandings because their children see many non-Chinese parents who hug and laugh easily.

Teenagers who grow up in Canada are likely to assert their independence. They believe in equality and personal rights, and demand the freedom to make their own decisions. Getting together with friends can become more important than being with family. Many parents, on the other hand, believe strongly in the family and demand obedience as a sign of respect. They may not understand how teenagers worry about being different and not belonging.

Expanding Chinese Churches

While Christian churches have been part of the Chinese-Canadian community since the turn of the century, the recent influxes of immigrants brought spectacular growth to Chinese Christian churches, especially in urban centres with large Chinese populations.

An estimated 8 percent of Hong Kong's population was Christian, but the growth of Chinese churches in Canada was accompanied by a high rate of new converts. In 1987, a Chinese Catholic parish was founded in Scarborough with 98 families totalling about 300 persons. By 1992, the parish had 1141 families with total membership of 3350. It had to use two high school halls for its Sunday masses. A new Chinese Catholic parish was planned to be established in Richmond Hill, near Toronto, where a significant population of Chinese-Canadians lived.

In 1993, there were 97 Protestant Chinese churches in the Greater Toronto area with a total membership of 19 000. The growth of these churches paralleled the waves of Hong Kong immigration. There was much cooperation between the Chinese Protestant denominations, which jointly issued a publication called Herald Monthly. It had a circulation of 70 000.

One reason for the growth of these churches was linked to immigration. With the insecurity and anxiety related to leaving home and starting life anew, people often searched for a deeper meaning in life. Religion could provide these meaning, as well as social support. Protestant churches were especially strong with activities such as fellowships, home visits, meetings for new immigrants and services for the elderly.

Another reason was linked to parental interest in providing their children with a good education. In Hong Kong, the missionary schools were renowned for their high standards. In Canada many parents were attracted to the Catholic faith by way of the separate school system.

Credit: Canada and Hong Kong Update. No. 11, Winter 1994.

The Issues of Race

In the fall of 1979, CTV's W5 newsmagazine ran a program called "Campus Giveaway" charging that foreigners were squeezing Canadian students out of Canadian universities. When the camera scanned a pharmacy class, it focused on Chinese faces. In fact, all the students shown were Canadian citizens. Chinese Canadians mounted a nation-wide protest and forced the television network to apologize for portraying Chinese as foreigners no matter how long they had lived in Canada.

Clearly, the media affected public attitudes towards immigrants and racial minorities. In the 1980s, many TV and newspaper reports described an "Asian invasion", focusing on the number of immigrants coming from Hong Kong and creating inaccurate images of Chinese Canadians. Among other things, these reports implied or indeed asserted that:

1. All Chinese immigrants were rich;
2. The Chinese were "taking over" the downtowns of Vancouver and Toronto by buying up office towers and hotels;
3. Chinese money was driving up house prices, especially in British Columbia;
4. Immigrants were a drain on the economy.

Zoning Battle

In 1992, the growing immigrant population in Vancouver found itself accused of being insensitive to the "character" of old, established neighbourhoods.

Shaughnessy was one of Vancouver's oldest, wealthiest districts, and many Chinese immigrants were buying property there and tearing down the older, English-cottage style houses. They then built much larger homes on the site with minimal lawns. In the late 1980s, homeowner organizations began to try to stop the growth of these larger new homes by calling for City Hall to zone for lower floor space ratios and for stricter design controls.

During public hearings held on this subject, City Hall discovered that long-standing residents wanted the zoning changes while the more recent residents, many from Hong Kong, opposed it.

On one hand, the new zoning proposals represented fears from long-term residents that their city was changing too rapidly. On the other hand, newer residents argued that the appropriate community "character" of Shaughnessy that the long-term residents wanted seemed to be based on assumptions of Anglo-Canadian identity. They felt the zoning amendments were not only directed at excluding large houses, but were also trying to exclude people arriving from Hong Kong.

To resolve the situation, Vancouver City Hall brought the contending sides together to work with city planners. Jointly, they prepared new zoning guidelines and new design controls that met the concerns of both sides. It took time and commitment from all parties involved, but a better understanding was achieved.

Credit: Canada and Hong Kong Update. No. 11, Winter 1994.

The Man from Montreal

In 1994, one of the most prominent of Montreal's 80 000 Chinese Canadians was Raymond Wong. That year, he received Concordia University's "Award of Distinction" that recognized his business skills and his community service.

In addition to volunteering time with Catholic organizations, Wong was president of the Chinese Community United Centre, the Chinese Botanical Gardens, and the Caisse Populaire (credit union) in Chinatown. He also served as honorary president of the organization "Adopted Children of China in Quebec." Overseas, he worked with schools and orphanages in China.

Wong headed Wing Wong Foods Incorporated, a family-owned business with its own extensive line of manufactured Chinese foods, including frozen egg rolls, spareribs, and sauces. The company is Canada's largest supplier of prepared Chinese foods and had almost 300 employees working in the east end of Montreal. Its products were distributed across Canada.

Wong's father, originally from Taishan county in South China, arrived in Canada in 1908. He married a French Canadian, and they had a family of eight children.

However, these allegations were not true. In reality,

1. Although middle-class professionals were arriving in Canada, even more new immigrants were working in the service industries and the garment trade because they did not speak an official language. Upon arrival, working-class immigrants rented modest homes and took menial jobs.

2. While capital from Hong Kong and Taiwan was indeed flowing into Canada, the actual number of buildings purchased by Asians was not high. Capital from Europe and the United States continued to dominate foreign investment in this country. As well, Canada welcomed foreign investment because it created jobs.

3. In British Columbia, house prices did go up partly because of a housing shortage. However, the shortage was caused by the large Canadian baby-boomer generation suddenly reaching house-buying age. Furthermore, migration into British Columbia by Canadians from other provinces was six times higher than migration from Hong Kong.

4. Statistics show that in 1990, immigrants to Canada since 1945, on average, paid more in taxes than they received in public services. Immigrants who entered after 1981 contributed a net of $10 000 to Canada, while those who entered between 1966 and 1970 contributed almost $20 000 more in taxes than they used in public services. As well, immigrants to Canada come with higher levels of education: of those who came between 1981 and 1991, 17 percent had a university degree, compared to 11 percent of their Canadian-born counterparts.

The negative reaction to Chinese immigration can be explained, in part, by past experience. Previously, immigrants usually entered Canada at the bottom of society. That is, most of them came in as poor and uneducated labourers who had little choice but to work at low-paying jobs.

But the Chinese from Hong Kong and Taiwan did not quite fit that pattern. While many were working-class, others were able to move immediately into professional jobs and middle-class suburbs. Also, because Chinese in general placed high value on education and were motivated to perform well, they provided a new source of competition that provoked envy and fear.

In the 1990s, there were calls to reduce the number of immigrants entering Canada, partly because of the prolonged recession. However, while central Canada (especially Ontario) suffered as a result of manufacturing jobs lost to the United States through Free Trade and industrial restructuring, the economy in British Columbia surged ahead, driven in part by the investments and spin-offs that accompanied Asian immigration.

Paper War

In 1993, *Ming Pao Daily News* launched its Toronto and Vancouver editions. It was the latest arrival in a long newspaper history in the Chinese community. *Ming Pao's* chief rival in Canada was the long-standing *Sing Tao,* another Hong Kong based newspaper, and not local Chinese newspapers that had been publishing in Canada since the turn of the century.

In Hong Kong, the parent operations of *Sing Tao* and *Ming Pao* newspapers published international editions. *Sing Tao,* for example, had fifteen separate daily editions published in Asia, North America, Australia and Europe.

These newspapers provided their readers with in-depth coverage of events happening in Hong Kong, China, Taiwan and other parts of Asia. As well, the Canadian editions of *Sing Tao* and *Ming Pao* carried several pages of Canadian political, economic and social news that had been edited locally. The Hong Kong, China and world news was produced in Hong Kong and transmitted electronically to Canada for the local editions.

In Canada, the readers of *Sing Tao* tended to be immigrants who had been here for at least three years. *Ming Pao* tried to carve its share of the reading market from the more newly arrived immigrants from Hong Kong.

In Vancouver, that city's edition of *Sing Tao* started in 1983 and had counterparts in New York, San Francisco, Los Angeles, London and Sydney. There were two pages in English, mostly about Asian business news and at least six reporters on its Vancouver staff. Often there were up to ten pages or more of local news.

In Toronto, each of the two major newspapers sold more than 30 000 copies daily in the 1990s. Editions ranged from 72 to 104 pages and carried a great deal of advertising, mostly from Chinese-Canadian businesses. Mainstream advertisers such as banks, airlines, insurance companies also bought space to reach the Chinese-Canadian market.

The Future

Amidst a shifting global economy, Canadian society is changing in ways that affect every single Canadian. Before 1961, 90 percent of immigrants who came to Canada were born in Europe. By 1991, Europe-born newcomers formed only 20 percent of Canada's immigrants, while those born in Asia represented almost 50 percent of the total. It is important to remember that change is never easy and is often hard to accept. But it is also important for Canadians to understand that the country needs immigrants to stop its population from shrinking. Then they will be less likely to fear the different faces around them.

Spadina Festival celebrating Canada Day, 1995, with the Boy Scouts, section 128.

Internationally, economic momentum is shifting towards the Pacific Rim. There, Asian economies are developing rapidly and becoming integrated into world markets. By the year 2000, it is estimated that 70 percent of world trade will involve the Pacific Rim. Immigrants from these regions, including Chinese, bring skills and connections that Canada can use to develop its competitiveness.

The Chinese in Canada are a diverse community. Their history in this country started before Confederation; there is continuing immigration from Asia; and there are ongoing issues around settlement and racism. All these elements challenge traditional notions of what Canada is and what its people will make of it.

Should Chinese be Credited?

In 1994, the University of British Columbia announced that it would no longer grant admission credits for Chinese- and Japanese-language courses taught at high schools but which were not provincially examined.

In British Columbia, Japanese was taught in 29 school districts and Mandarin Chinese was taught in 11. Over 10 000 secondary school students, mostly in the Greater Vancouver area, studied one of the two languages.

Although there was growing demand for Chinese-and Japanese-language classes, they were not included in the provincial exams. However, at the same time, French, Spanish, Latin and German were included in the provincial exams.

In reaction to the decision of the University of British Columbia, the Chinese Language Education Advancement Coalition of British Columbia was formed among many community groups. Its main goal was to pressure the Ministry of Education to include Chinese and Japanese as approved subjects for provincial examination and to have the University of British Columbia accept the two languages as subjects in determining admission.

The issue resolved with Mandarin Chinese being added to the list of subjects to be provincially examinable. This meant the credits could be used for admitting students to the University of British Columbia.

Credit: Canada and Hong Kong Update. No. 12, Spring 1994.

Chapter Nine

Some People to Meet

Chinese Canadians work in almost every trade and profession in Canada. This section introduces some of those who have made significant achievements in their chosen field.

Adrienne Clarkson, O.C.

Arts

Wayne Ngan is one of Canada's most admired potters. He is the first living potter to have a piece accepted by Taiwan's National Palace Museum. In 1983, he won the $15 000 Saidye Bronfman Award for Excellence in Canadian Craftsmanship.

Wayne was born in Canton, China, and came to Canada in 1951. He studied at the Vancouver School of Art and currently lives on Hornby Island, off the British Columbia coast, where he works natural materials (such as seaweed and ashes) into his pots. He says, "When I look out at all the nature around me, it becomes my pottery. It is very pleasing: all things become part of you."

Architecture

Bing Thom designed the Canadian pavilion for the 1992 World's Fair in Seville, Spain. The pavilion was six storeys high and 76 metres long. "It's big, it's quiet," says Bing. "To me, that's Canada. We're not flashy people, but we're here." He also designed five pavilions for Expo 86 in Vancouver, including those for the Northwest Territories and Hong Kong.

Bing is a third-generation Canadian, whose grandfather was a pioneer missionary preaching at Christian missions throughout western Canada. He worked closely with another famous Canadian architect, Arthur Erickson, for twenty years before starting his own firm.

Broadcasting

Adrienne Clarkson was born in Hong Kong but came to Canada at the age of two. In 1965, she started her television career as the book reviewer on the program *Take 30*. She went on to host the show until 1973, interviewing celebrities from around the world. During that time, she also published two novels. In 1976 she became host of the newsmagazine program *Fifth Estate*. She won ACTRA awards in 1973, 1974, 1975 and 1981.

In 1982, Adrienne was appointed Agent-General for Ontario in Paris. Four years later, she became the publisher, president and chief executive officer of McClelland and Stewart, the noted Canadian publishing house. In 1988 she returned to television to produce and host *Adrienne Clarkson Presents*, a prime-time arts program. In the 1990s, she began to direct her own feature films. She is the recipient of three honourary doctorates and in October, 1992 was appointed an officer of the Order of Canada.

Business

Canadian design superstar **Alfred Sung,** of Club Monaco fame, has created more than 17 product lines. These include fashion lines for men, women and children, luggage, perfume, furs and household linens. His products are sold around the world.

Alfred was born in Shanghai, raised in Hong Kong, and studied fashion design in France. "I was only seventeen at the time," Alfred recalls. "I definitely knew I didn't want to be a dentist, a lawyer or a doctor. I was delighted to take fashion design because I could still draw and paint and use crayons."

He moved to Toronto and opened his first boutique there in 1976.

In 1985, **Kwok Yuen Ho** founded ATI Technologies Inc., which became a world leader in computer graphics boards. The boards developed by ATI sped up the computer's ability to handle graphic information, displayed high-resolution pictures and let the computer do video-editing.

Alfred Sung

Keith Lock on location directing his feature film, Small Pleasures.

Mina Shum

ATI challenged the industry practice of manufacturing products in Asia by keeping production based at its Toronto plant, which employed 400 workers.

"If we manufacture in the Far East, the product has to be shipped over, assembled and then shipped back for testing," said Henry Quan, Vice-President of Marketing. "Over here we can change production lines in a day if we wish."

Film

Keith Lock was born in Toronto in 1951 and grew up working in his family's pharmacy in Chinatown. He began making films in 1973. His 1986 film *A Brighter Moon* was nominated for a Gemini Award, and his feature *Small Pleasures* made its debut at the Toronto International Film Festival in 1993.

Brenda Lem is a writer, artist and filmmaker born and raised in Toronto. Her films have been shown in festivals in Los Angeles, New York, Hong Kong and across Canada. Her films include *The Company* (1990) and *Open Letter: Grasp the Bird's Tail* (1992).

When **Mina Shum's** first feature film *Double Happiness* premiered at the Toronto International Film Festival in 1994, it won a special citation from the jury choosing the best Canadian film. At the Berlin International Film Festival in 1995, the same film won the prize for Best First Film. The film tells the story of Jade Li, a young Chinese Canadian struggling to be an actress.

Mina studied theatre at the University of British Columbia and then received a film diploma. She made several short films, including *Me, Mom and Mona*, which won a prize at the 1993 Toronto International Film Festival.

Mina was born in Hong Kong and came to Canada as a child with her parents. About her father, she said, "… I've come to understand the difficulty of coming to a new country where your education means nothing, humbling yourself, dealing with racism. He had to deal with that and he had to raise his family with a sure hand."

Music

Alexina Louie is one of very few composers to make a living from their work. In 1986, she was named Composer of the Year by the Canadian Music Council and in 1992, she won an award for the Most Performed Canadian Composer.

As a child growing up in Vancouver's Chinatown, Alexina was "painfully shy." She started studying piano at the age of seven, and went on to study music at the University of British Columbia and in the United States. She has more than twenty-five commissioned works to her credit, and her compositions have been performed by symphonies across Canada and in Europe.

The music director for the Toronto Symphony once said, "Louie writes for orchestra with great flair – and makes orchestras sound brilliant."

Sook-Yin Lee was the lead singer and lyricist of the band Bob's Your Uncle. In 1989, it was one of four bands selected to perform at the annual New Music Seminar in New York. That resulted in a California company signing the band to a deal. Bob's Your Uncle has since released a mini-LP, a cassette single, and an LP. The band has been described as "a bright, imaginative breath of fresh air."

Sook-Yin also made a short film for the National Film Board where she was writer, director, musician, actor and producer. As a child, she put on shows for the neighbourhood kids. "I remember asking all the kids to close their eyes. While their eyes were closed I was playing my nose. The kids really thought I was playing Hawaiian guitars."

In 1994, MuchMusic, the national music TV station, hired Sook-Yin as a video jockey. She hosted a daily show called *The Wedge*. That year, Sook Yin also released her solo album *Lavinia's Tongue*.

On location during the filming of Double Happiness, *directed by Mina Shum, with actors, left to right, Stephen Chang, Alannah Ong, Sandra Oh, and Frances You.*

Sook-Yin Lee

Politics

The first Chinese Canadian elected to Parliament was **Douglas Jung,** who represented Vancouver Centre from 1957 to 1962. During his term, he also represented Canada at the United Nations. He was followed by **Art Lee,** an Alberta-born lawyer who was practising in Vancouver, elected in 1974. **Raymond Chan,** from Hong Kong, was elected in 1993 and named Secretary of State for Asia and the Pacific.

Bob Wong, born in Fort Erie, Ontario, won a seat in the Ontario Legislature in 1987. He was the first Chinese to be named to a cabinet in Canada, serving as Minister of Energy and Minster of Culture and Citizenship.

Sandra Wilking grew up in South Africa but came to Vancouver via Hong Kong. She was elected to Vancouver City Council in 1988, where **Bill Yee** had been elected previously in 1982. Vancouver's first Chinese School Trustee was **Jack Say Yee,** elected in 1973.

Olivia Chow from Hong Kong studied sculpture at the Ontario College of Arts before being elected as a Toronto School Board trustee and then as a Metropolitan Toronto councillor. Her colleague, **Tam Goosen,** was also from Hong Kong and also served as a Toronto School Board trustee.

In the Prairie provinces, **George Ho Lem** served as Calgary alderman from 1959 to 1962, while **Wayne Mah** was alderman (1982–1984), then mayor (1984–1985) of Eston, Saskatchewan. **Ken Wong** was elected alderman in Winnipeg in 1972.

Peter Wong was elected mayor of Sudbury, Ontario, in 1983 and **Peter Wing** was mayor of Kamloops, British Columbia, from 1966 to 1971, after serving as alderman for three terms. In Saanich, British Columbia. **Ed Lum** served as alderman from 1965 to 1973 and as mayor from 1974 to 1977.

David Lam, former Lieutenant-Governor of British Columbia

Public Service

Susan Eng was a tax lawyer who had been active in community politics since 1980 when she was appointed to the Ontario Premier's Council on Technology and Change in 1989. Between 1991–1995 she served as Chair of the Metropolitan Toronto Police Services Board, which oversees the 6000-member police force.

Dr. Joseph Wong was born in Hong Kong but came to Canada in 1968 and earned an electrical engineering degree at McGill University. He then went on to study medicine in New York and started his own practice in Toronto in 1982. He soon became an energetic and influential community leader.

In 1983, Dr. Wong organized the first United Way walkathon in the Chinese community. Three hundred people took part and raised $17 000. The walkathon has since expanded to include all people, and has raised a record $360 000. In 1990, Dr. Wong was chairman of the United Way of Greater Toronto, and in 1993 he was named to the Order of Canada. That same year, he received the Canadian Council of Christians and Jews Humanitarian Award for his many years of community service including volunteer work related to Southeast Asian refugees, medical research, a geriatric care centre, and the Chinese Canadian National Council.

Winnie Ng, who came from Hong Kong as a student, became Executive Assistant to the Ontario Minister of Citizenship in 1990. She was a union organizer for Chinese garment workers and helped improve working conditions for immigrant women with a mobile health unit, a daycare centre, and English-in-the-Workplace programs. In May 1992, she ran for Parliament in downtown Toronto.

David Lam was known as a philanthropist who gave a million dollars each to the University of British Columbia, the University of Victoria and Christian Regent College.

He was a banker in Hong Kong before immigrating to Canada in 1967, where he worked in real estate. "People from Hong Kong bring entrepreneurship and a hard-working spirit,"

Dr. Tak Mak

he has said. "But whether the Oriental presence is going to be easily accepted is another matter. One can easily legislate against discrimination, but no one can legislate love." In 1988, he was appointed Lieutenant-Governor of British Columbia and served until 1995.

Science

Tak Mak is Canada's top scientist studying the immune system. He won recognition in 1984 for figuring out the structure of the T-cell receptor, a key element in the immune system.

Raised in Hong Honk, Tak moved with his family to America when he was a teenager. He worked at the Ontario Cancer Institute for many years.

In 1993, he was named head of a new research institute of seventy scientists financed at $10 million a year by a major pharmaceutical company.

Another scientist, **Lap Chee Tsui** of the University of Toronto, received the Order of Canada for his work in identifying the gene that causes fibrosis, one of the most common life-threatening inherited diseases.

Lap Chee was born in China and came to the University of Toronto to work with a geneticist at the Hospital for Sick Children.

Larry Wang came to Alberta in 1971 to study squirrels. Twenty years later, he invented the Canadian Cold Buster Bar, sold across Canada and in Asia.

Larry's research focused on the fact that gophers live off their own body fat for six to eight months a year, whereas humans produce a chemical that prevents body fat from changing into energy. He discovered natural ingredients that blocked that chemical, thereby helping humans retain body heat longer. That was the secret formula to his Cold Buster Bar.

Born in China, Larry grew up in Taiwan and studied in Texas. He was elected to the Royal Society of Canada for his work, and is very keen on science. "The next century will be a technology race," he said, "and advanced science will drive the economy."

Normie Kwong

Albert Chang

Sports

Normie Kwong, nicknamed "The China Clipper," played on four Grey Cup championship teams (Calgary Stampeders 1948, Edmonton Eskimos 1954-1956). As fullback, he set thirty Canadian Football League individual records and was the first CFL player to rush for over 9 000 yards. He was selected All-Canadian Fullback five times, and won the Schenley Award as Most Outstanding Canadian Player in 1955 and 1956. In 1955, he was selected as Canada's Athlete of the Year.

The only Chinese Canadian to have played in the National Hockey League was **Larry Kwong** (no relation to Normie). After being discharged from the Army, Larry was signed to play for the New York Rangers for the 1946-1947 season.

Lori Fung won a gold medal in rhythmic gymnastics at the 1984 Olympics. From Vancouver, Lori dropped out of school and took her grade 12 by correspondence while she trained. When she won her medal, she recalled, "I never had time for a social life or parties in high school, and none of my friends could understand me. But the other day I received a good luck card signed by a lot of the kids I knew in school but whom I hadn't seen in years. They realized that dream of mine wasn't so stupid after all."

Susanna Yuen of Winnipeg started skating at age seven, and in 1990 played right wing on Canada's national women's team, the first-ever world champions. As a university student, she worked part-time in the family business, Peking Chinese Food, and also played in the women's city league and coached a rural twelve-year-old boys team.

Tennis player **Albert Chang** was born in Vancouver in 1971 and was a member of Canada's World Youth Cup team in 1987-88. He was named to the 1992, 1994 and 1995 Davis Cup teams. Among his many career triumphs are winning the 1994 Celle Challenger (Singles) and 1994 Manila Challenger (Doubles) matches. In 1994, he was ranked number 3 in Canada and his prize money for that year was over $65 000. He graduated in pre-medicine from Harvard University in 1992.

Writers

SKY Lee

Evelyn Lau

The cover of SKY Lee's book Bellydancer.

SKY Lee's first novel *Disappearing Moon Cafe*, was nominated for a Governor General's Award when it was published in 1990. Born in Port Alberni, British Columbia, SKY earned a B.A. in Fine Arts from the University of British Columbia as well as a Diploma in Nursing from Douglas College. Her short stories have been published in numerous periodicals, and she also illustrated a children's book, *Teach me to Fly, Skyfighter.*

"I'm not very kind to a lot of the woman-hating that goes on, not only in Chinatown, but in every culture," SKY declared. She is also aware of many issues connected with writing. "Our original cultural voice was lost in the process of being displaced from China to Canada. I'm often ashamed to say that my voice is in my colonizer's language in English."

Winston Kam was born in Port-of-Spain, Trinidad, and now lives in Toronto. He has written several plays, including *Bachelor Men, Letters to Wu* and *Les Vampyrs Extant.*

The cover of the book Oedipal Dreams, by Evelyn Lau.

Evelyn Lau's book *Runaway: Diary of a Street Kid* topped the paperback bestseller list in 1989 and has been made into a CBC movie. Her second book of poetry, *Oedipal Dreams* (1992), was nominated for the Governor General's Award.

Evelyn was born in Vancouver and began to have her poems

published in literary magazines when she was thirteen years old. "I just knew, at the age of six, I would be a writer," she recalls, "and nothing was going to stop me. I was so frustrated because no one appreciated the single-mindedness I had about it."

Fred Wah was born in Swift Current, Saskatchewan, and grew up in the Kootenay region of British Columbia. His book *Waiting for Saskatchewan* won the Governor General's Award for Poetry in 1985. He has published eleven books and teaches creative writing at the University of Calgary.

The cover of Fred Wah's book Alley Alley Home Free.

"I'm one-quarter Chinese," Fred has said. "Most kids of any ethnic identity have to deal with some ethnic slur, and it certainly was there in my life, but I don't harbour any ill will toward anyone about that. A lot of Canadians know the feeling of not being racially pure, particularly growing up and not being able to say 'I'm Canadian.'"

Denise Chong was born in Vancouver and grew up in Prince George, British Columbia. Trained as an economist, she worked in the federal Department of Finance as a western affairs adviser. She later became an economic advisor to former Prime Minister Pierre Trudeau.

After working in China for two years in the mid-1990s, she became a freelance writer. Her first book, *The Concubine's Children*, was published in 1994 and was nominated for the Governor General's Literary Award. The vividly written book takes the reader into the history of Denise's family in Canada and in China.

Fred Wah

Chronology:

The Chinese in Canada

1788   John Meares arrives in Nootka Sound on Canada's Pacific coast, with two ships and 50 Chinese carpenters and craftsmen. They build a two-storied fort and a schooner, but are later captured by the Spanish and taken to Mexico.

1858   The first Chinese gold-miners arrive in British Columbia from San Francisco.

1860   The first Chinese woman lands in Victoria, B.C. She is the wife of the owner of the Kwong Lee Company.

1861   Won Alexander Cumyow is born at Port Douglas, B.C. He is the first Chinese born in Canada.

1866   The first cargo of timber shipped to China leaves Burrard Inlet (later Vancouver) for Shanghai.

1872   British Columbia passes a law to disqualify Chinese from voting.

1877   Chinese-owned laundries are established in Toronto.

1881   The Canadian Pacific Railway contractor Andrew Onderdonk starts to hire Chinese labourers for railway work.

1883   The Methodist Home for Chinese Girls opens in Victoria to help those escaping prostitution, slavery or marriage contracts.

1885   Completion of the Canadian Pacific Railway. The federal government levies a $50 head tax on Chinese immigrants entering Canada.

1891   Vancouver's Reverend Chan Sing Kai is the first Chinese minister ordained by the Methodist Church.

1892   A smallpox alarm in Calgary leads to destruction of Chinese laundries by a mob of 300.

1894   The Presbyterian Church starts missionary work among the Chinese in Toronto.

1895   The Sino-Japanese War ends in a shocking defeat for China. Reform leaders appeal to overseas Chinese for help to modernize and strengthen China.

       Chinese Board of Trade formed in Vancouver.

       Feng Choy opens one of Halifax's first Chinese-owned laundries.

1902	Royal Commission on Chinese and Japanese Immigration holds hearings and concludes that limiting Chinese immigration will not damage trade between China and Canada. The head tax is raised to $100.
1903	The head tax is raised to $500.
1906	Newfoundland passes a law requiring all Chinese immigrants to pay a head tax of $300.
1907	Anti-Asian riots sweep through Vancouver's Chinatown, causing $26 000 in damages.
1910	The City of Hamilton passes by-laws against Chinese-owned laundries.
	The Chinese population in Quebec City is estimated to be 60.
1911	Dr. Sun Yat-sen visits Canada to raise funds for the revolution that topples the Ching dynasty.
1912	The Province of Saskatchewan bans employment of White women in Chinese-owned laundries and restaurants. Chinese challenge the law in the courts, but the ruling favours the province.
1916	The Chinese Labour Association is organized in British Columbia.
1917	Toronto's YMCI (Young Men's Christian Institute) holds the first conference of Chinese students in Canada.
	Employers in British Columbia, Alberta and Saskatchewan propose importing Chinese workers to relieve the labour shortage caused by the First World War.
1919	A missionary report notes that Vancouver has 6000 Chinese with 210 families, and Toronto has 2100 Chinese with 35 families.
1920	A dozen Chinese veterans who served in the Canadian Army during the First World War are given the right to vote.
1921	A Montreal newspaper reports that the city's Chinese population is about 1600, with 600 businesses.
1923	The federal government passes the Chinese Immigration Act, banning Chinese immigration.
1931	During the Great Depression, the Anglican Church sets up a soup kitchen in Vancouver's Chinatown, where 80 percent of the people are unemployed.

1932   The Chinese Aero Club is formed: member pilots later return to China.

1936   *The Chinese News Weekly,* an English-language newspaper, begins publication in Vancouver.

1937   The Chinese Tennis Club is organized in Vancouver.

1939   The Second World War begins. Five hundred Chinese men serve in the Canadian Army. Chinese Canadians work in war industries, and soon the Dock and Shipyard Workers Union has 300 Chinese members and several Chinese stewards. Later, the International Woodworkers of America appoints its first full-time Chinese union organizer.

1941   Vancouver's Chinese set up their own Air Raid Patrol and train 100 wardens.

1942   Roger Chen is the first Chinese Canadian to be commissioned in the Canadian Army.

1945   The Second World War ends. The racial bar against Chinese is lifted at Vancouver's Crystal Pool, a public swimming pool.

1947   The Chinese Immigration Act is repealed and limited entry of wives and children of Chinese Canadians starts.

Chinese in British Columbia are allowed to vote and to work as pharmacists, lawyers, and accountants.

1950   The Korean Conflict starts. Canada is part of the United Nations force assisting South Korea, which is in conflict with North Korea. China supports North Korea.

1953   The first Chinatown Lions Club in North America is formed in Vancouver.

1955   Margaret Gee is the first Chinese-Canadian woman lawyer called to the bar.

1957   Douglas Jung is the first Chinese Canadian elected to the federal Parliament.

1961   Canada sells $362 million in wheat to China.

1967   The introduction of a "point system" to Canadian immigration marks the beginning of a new era of Chinese entries.

1970   Canada establishes diplomatic ties with the People's Republic of China.

1971   Vancouver's Chinatown is designated a historic site.

1973 A special immigration provision grants permanent residency to Chinese students and visitors who came to Canada prior to November 1972.

1975 A Chinese-Canadian Youth Conference is held in Vancouver on the themes of "Identity and Awareness."

1979 CTV airs *Campus Giveaway* program, which sparks nation-wide protests in the Chinese community. This leads to formation of the Chinese Canadian National Council (CCNC).

1980 The first building of the Chinese Cultural Centre complex in Vancouver opens.

1983 Chinese Canadians celebrate the 125th anniversary of Chinese settlement in Canada.

1984 The Vancouver Art Gallery presents the exhibition "Gum San: Images of Gold Mountain, 1886-1947."

The Chinese Canadian National Council launches a campaign to get redress from the Canadian government for past payments of the head tax by Chinese immigrants.

1986 Dr. Sun Yat-sen Garden and Park opens as the only full-scale classical Chinese garden outside China. It becomes a major tourist attraction for Vancouver.

Jim Wong-Chu's *Chinatown Ghosts* is the first book of poetry published in English by an immigrant Chinese Canadian.

1989 The multi-media exhibition "Beyond the Golden Mountain" on Chinese-Canadian history and culture opens at the Canadian Museum of Civilization in Ottawa.

1990 The Toronto Association for Democracy in China is incorporated.

1991 *Many Mouthed Birds,* an anthology of contemporary writing by Chinese Canadians, is published.

1993 Vancouver law firm Boughton, Peterson, Yang & Anderson becomes the first foreign firm to obtain an official licence to practice law in China.

Todd Wong, a fifth-generation Chinese Canadian, wins the Terry Fox Medal for Simon Fraser University at age 33 for his personal battle with cancer and for his efforts to create racial harmony.

Member of Parliament Raymond Chan (born in Hong Kong) is appointed Secretary of State for Asia Pacific affairs and becomes the first Chinese Canadian to sit on the federal Privy Council.

Member of the Legislative Assembly Gary Mar, a third generation Chinese Canadian, is appointed to the Alberta cabinet as Minister of Community Development.

1994 The Canada-Hong Kong Resource Centre is established at the University of Toronto as part of the Joint Centre for Asia Pacific Studies. The Centre, open to the public, will serve as an archive for Hong Kong immigrant communities in Canada and include a research collection on Canada-Hong Kong relations and developments in Hong Kong before and after 1997. The Hong Kong Bank of Canada donates $500 000 for the Centre.

Thirty Chinese Canadians run for public office in the Greater Toronto Area local elections.

The federal government rejects a call for redress on Chinese head tax.

1995 Eighth annual Chinese Film Festival in Canada.

Mina Shum's film, *Double Happiness* wins the prize for Best First Film at the Berlin International Film Festival.

Immigration Law:
- pg. 52, pg. 53

The Community
Today
- pg. 63,

Chronology
pg. 82, 83, 84, 85, 86,

Chronology:

The Chinese throughout History

1766-1122 BC During China's first dynasty, the Shang, the Chinese develop horse-drawn chariots and a system of writing.

300 BC Chinese army commanders use magnetic compass for military purposes.

221-206 BC During the Qin dynasty, the Emperor starts building the Great Wall of China. Over the centuries, construction continues under different rulers. The Great Wall is 6400 kilometres in length and it is the longest structure ever built by human beings.

AD 105 Chinese invent paper. The Arabs learn from them how to make paper and take it to Europe in the 12th Century.

550 Silk, developed by the Chinese over a thousand years earlier, comes to the West.

1126 First detailed description of the use of gunpowder, invented by the Chinese, in a battle.

1215 Genghis Khan, a chief of northern Mongol tribes, seizes Beijing, the capital of China. By 1227, he controls lands reaching from Beijing to the Caspian Sea.

1275 Marco Polo from Venice visits China and travels widely through the country for the next 16 years.

1405 Admiral Chen Ho leads the first of seven naval expeditions into the waters of Southeast Asia and the Indian Ocean. Chinese ships go as far as Java, (now Indonesia) southern India, the Persian Gulf and East Africa.

1514 Portuguese ships arrive off the coast of south China, but are not allowed to land.

1603 Spanish army kills 23 000 Chinese in the Philippines after an uprising.

1639 Chinese farmers revolt against the Spanish in the Philippines. In Luzon, 22 000 Chinese are killed and another 7000 surrender.

1644 The Ming dynasty ends in China as Manchu invaders seize the throne. Ming loyalists set up a rebel base on Taiwan.

1740	Dutch authorities in Java provoke an armed uprising by deciding to deport unemployed Chinese. Ten thousand Chinese are killed in one week in Batavia.
1757	China opens one port (Canton) to trade with the West.
1780	Chinese arrive in Mauritius (an island off southeast Africa) to work as carpenters, tailors, blacksmiths and sugar plantation labourers.
1810	Chinese tea growers arrive in Brazil.
1819	Singapore is established as a trading post of the British East India Company.
1821	Chinese in Thailand have a fleet of 136 ships which trade with China, Vietnam, Malaya and Java.
1821	Direct migration from China to Singapore begins.
1833	Great Britain's Emancipation Act frees Black slaves in its empire. Colonial farmers and mine-owners are left without cheap labour. This leads to the use of indentured workers (contract labourers) from China.
1841	The colony of Hong Kong is founded.
1842	Hong Kong is ceded to Britain when China is defeated in the First Opium War.
1847	Chinese labourers are taken to Cuba to work on sugar plantations. From 1847 to 1873, 143 000 Chinese make the journey, but many die on the way.
1849	Start of Chinese immigration to Peru. From 1849 to 1874, 90 000 Chinese are shipped there.
1851	Gold is discovered in Australia. Fifty thousand Chinese arrive in Australia in the decade and work as miners and labourers.
1852	Twenty thousand Chinese arrive in California for the gold rush there.
1852	Chinese contract workers arrive in Hawaii.
1853	Chinese contract workers start to arrive in Trinidad and British Guiana.
1854	Chinese contract workers are introduced in Jamaica.
1856	California imposes a "Foreign Miners Tax" on the Chinese gold miners.
1860	California passes a law allowing segregated schools for non-Whites.

Chinese labourers work in the silver mines in Nevada.

1861 Gold is discovered in New Zealand.

1865 The Central Pacific Railroad in the United States starts using Chinese workers. By 1868, 12 000 Chinese are helping to build the transcontinental line.

1867 Singapore becomes a British colony.

1870 Indonesia has 250 000 Chinese, about one percent of the total population.

1871 Salmon canneries in the Pacific Northwest start using Chinese workers.

1872 Twenty-five thousand Chinese tin miners are working in Perak province in Malaya.

1874 Peru passes legislation to stop Chinese workers from entering.

1876 The Chinese population in the Philippines reaches 30 000.

1876 Cuba grants freedom to 43 000 Chinese coolies.

1877 China establishes diplomatic relations with Britain.

1880 By this date, six percent of farmers in California are Chinese.

1881 Over 600 Chinese live in British ports, such as London, Liverpool, Bristol and Glasgow. The Chinese people operate laundries, grocery stores, restaurants and rooming-houses.

1882 The United States starts restricting Chinese immigration.

1885 Twenty-eight Chinese are murdered in Rock Springs, Wyoming, during anti-Chinese riots.

1897 Chinese arrive in Madagascar, which becomes the third largest Chinese community in Africa.

1897 Natal, South Africa, bans Chinese immigration.

1900 In June the Boxer Rebellion begins in North China. Secret societies rebel against invasion by foreigners.

1901 Australia passes Immigration Restriction Act.

1904 Ten thousand Chinese contract workers arrive in South Africa to work in gold mines.

1904 The United States stops immigration of Chinese workers.

1911	The Ching dynasty is overthrown; the Republic of China begins.
1912	A Chinese Y.M.C.A. is established in the United States.
1917	Two hundred thousand Chinese are brought to France as workers to help the Allies in the First World War.
1920	New Zealand stops Chinese immigration.
1921	Dr. Sun Yat-sen becomes president of a new revolutionary government based in Canton, South China.
	The Chinese Communist Party is founded.
1925	Dr. Sun Yat-sen, regarded by many as the "Father of Modern China," dies and is succeeded by Chiang Kai-shek.
1931	Chinese in Malaya form 39 percent of the total population.
1932	Chinese form 12 percent of the population in Thailand and 1.6 percent in French Indochina and Burma. They own 90 percent of rice mills in Thailand and 80 percent in Vietnam.
1934	The communist Chinese Red Army of over 90 000 soldiers begins its "Long March" of nearly 6000 miles (3500 kilometres), pursued by the armies of the Nationalist government. A year later, seven to eight thousand survive to trek into Shaanxi province in northern China. There, the Communists recruit new strength.
1941	The United States enters the Second World War. Eight thousand Chinese Americans enlist for military services.
1943	American anti-Chinese immigration laws are repealed.
1948	Start of the "Malaysian Emergency," which eventually leads to 10 000 Chinese being repatriated to China between 1950 and 1952.
1949	Australia passes a law to deport Asian (mostly Chinese) wartime refugees.
	Mao Zedong becomes China's first Communist chairman, ruling China for the next 27 years.
	The People's Republic of China is established on Taiwan with Taipei as the "temporary capital". Chiang Kai-Shek is the first president from 1950 until his death in 1975.

Refugees flee to Hong Kong (population 2 million). Among the newcomers are Shanghai industrialists who bring new capital and entrepreneurial skills to the colony.

1950   The Korean Conflict starts. A United Nations embargo on trade with China forces Hong Kong to transform itself from a shipping centre to a manufacturing centre.

1952   Land reform undertaken in China.

1954   French colonialists depart from Vietnam.

1956   Chinese nationals in southern Vietnam are forbidden by law to enter eleven important occupations.

1958   China shells Nationalist positions in the Taiwan Straits.

1960   Ships transport over 100 000 Chinese to China from Indonesia, where anti-Chinese agitation is rising.

1962   War breaks out between China and India. China sends ships to transport Chinese back home.

1962   China lets 70 000 illegal immigrants cross the border into Hong Kong. Hong Kong tries to keep them out.

1965   First American air strikes against North Vietnam.

1965   Singapore becomes a sovereign and independent nation.

1966   The Cultural Revolution brings chaos to China as Chairman Mao seeks to maintain his control over the country. Red Guards are unleashed.

1966   Anti-Chinese sentiment in Indonesia culminates in hundreds of Chinese killed. There is mob violence, extortion and harassment. Ten thousand Chinese head for China.

1967   The Cultural Revolution leads to riots in Hong Kong.

1969   Fighting breaks out between Malays and Chinese in Malaysia. Two hundred die, 400 are wounded and much property is damaged.

1970   Singapore's population of two million is 75 percent Chinese, 15 percent Malaysian, and 8 percent Indian.

1970   China and Canada establish diplomatic relations.

1970   War in Vietnam spreads to Cambodia.

1971   The People's Republic of China gets official recognition by the United Nations and un-seats Taiwan (Republic of China)

1971   Peru is estimated to have 30 000 Chinese-born Chinese and 300 000 Peruvian Chinese.

1973   The "White Australia" policy comes to an end. Australia has 30 000 Chinese, of whom 10 000 are foreign students or others on temporary permits.

1975   Communists seize control of Phnom Penh, capital of Cambodia (now Kampuchea). Half of Cambodia's Chinese population of 400 000 are killed.

         "Boat People" start to flee South Vietnam. Seventy thousand of these people arrive in Hong Kong in the following years.

1976   Chairman Mao Zedong dies, and extremist are purged from political power.

1984   Britain signs an agreement to return Hong Kong to China in 1997.

1989   At Tiananmen Square, in Beijing, one million Chinese protest the lack of democracy in China. Troops open fire killing hundreds of demonstrators.

         Michael Chang, an American tennis player, age 17, wins the French Open and becomes the youngest male winner of a Grand Slam title in tennis history.

1991   Hong Kong's first-ever legislative council election takes place. The United Democrats take most of the eighteen seats; all three pro-China candidates are defeated.

1992   In China, forty political dissidents are arrested.

         By the end of 1992, there are 8700 "economic development zones" in China, up from 117 at the year's beginning.

1993   Hong Kong manufacturers employ 3 million workers in China, equal to more than half of Hong Kong's total population of 5.8 million.

         Manufacturers' Life Insurance Company of Toronto opens its first office in China.

         Taiwan begins a push to rejoin the United Nations.

         Ang Lee's film *The Wedding Banquet* (a Taiwan-USA co-production) about a gay Chinese-American wins the Golden Bear award at the Berlin Film Festival.

         Amy Tan's novel *The Joy Luck Club*, about Chinese immigrant women to America and their daughters, is made into a major Hollywood film, with Oliver Stone producing and Wayne Wang directing.

1994   Canadian Prime Minister Jean Chrétien leads a delegation of nine provincial premiers ("Team Canada") on a trade visit to China.

The International Monetary Fund (IMF) ranks China as the world's third largest economy, behind the US and Japan.

1995   China's Chen Lu wins the gold medal at the World Figure Skating Championship.

Wei Jingsheng, China's prominent advocate of democracy is sentenced to fourteen years in prison for conspiring to subvert the government. In 1993 he had been released from prison after nearly fifteen years for agitating to overthrow the government.

Further Reading

Chan, Anthony, *Gold Mountain: The Chinese in the New World.* Vancouver: New Star, 1982.

Chinese Canadian National Council, Women's Book Committee, *Jin Guo: Voices of Chinese Canadian Women.* Toronto: Toronto Women's Press, 1992.

Chong, Denise, *The Concubine's Children: Portrait of a Family Divided.* Toronto: Penguin Books, 1994.

Con, Harry et. al., *From China to Canada: A History of the Chinese Communities in Canada.* Toronto: McClelland & Stewart, 1982.

Harris, Heather and Mary Sun, *The Chinese Canadians.* Toronto: Nelson Canada, 1982.

Hoe, Ban Seng, *Beyond the Golden Mountain: Chinese Cultural Traditions in Canada.* Ottawa: Canadian Museum of Civilization, 1989.

Huang, Evelyn with Lawrence Jeffrey, *Voices from a Community.* Vancouver: Douglas & McIntyre, 1992.

Lai, David Chuen-Yan, *Chinatown: Towns Within Cities.* Vancouver: University of British Columbia Press, 1988.

Lee, Bennett and Jim Wong-Chu, *Many-Mouthed Birds: Contemporary Writing by Chinese Canadians.* Vancouver & Toronto: Douglas & McIntyre, 1991.

Nipp, Dora, "The Chinese in Toronto," in Robert F. Harney, ed., *Gathering Places.* Toronto: Multicultural History Society of Ontario, 1985.

Tan, Jin and Roy, Patricia, *The Chinese in Canada.* Ottawa: Canadian Historical Association, 1985.

Tepper, Elliot L., *Southeast Asia Exodus: From Transition to Resettlement.* Ottawa: Canadian Asian Studies Association, 1980.

Welldon, Christine, *Canadian Pacific Railway: Pon Git Chong.* Toronto: Grolier Ltd., 1991.

Wright, Richard Thomas, *In a Strange Land: A Pictorial Record of the Chinese in Canada, 1788-1923.* Saskatoon: Western Producer Prairie Books, 1988.

Yee, Paul, *Breakaway.* Toronto: Groundwood, 1994. (Juvenile Fiction).

_____, *The Curses of Third Uncle.* Toronto: James Lorimer and Company, 1986. (Juvenile Fiction).

_____, *Roses Sing on New Snow.* Toronto: Groundwood, 1991. (Picture Book).

_____, *Saltwater City: The Chinese in Vancouver.* Vancouver: Douglas & McIntyre, 1988.

_____, *Tales from Gold Mountain: The Chinese in the New World.* Toronto: Groundwood, 1989.

_____, *Teach Me to Fly, Skyfighter.* Toronto: James Lorimer and Company, 1983. (Juvenile Fiction).

Picture Acknowledgements

The cooperation of persons and organizations in providing photographs and permission to reproduce them is gratefully appreciated.

11 Vancouver Public Library, #12866 13
Provincial Archives of British Columbia; 14
Vancouver Public Library; #13270 16 top
Notman Photographic Archives Archives,
#MP013/79, McCord Museum of McGill
University; bottom Notman Photographic
Archives, #2117 VIEW, McCord Museum of
McGill University; 17 top Provincial
Archives of British Columbia, #75088,
Onderdonk Collection; middle Glenbow
Archives, NA-1604-82; bottom Province of
British Columbia Archives, HP 72553; 18
Notman Photographic Archives #26,231-I,
McCord Museum of McGill University; 19
Manitoba Chinese Historical Society; 21

Saskatchewan Archives Board; 23 Revised
Statutes of British Columbia; 25 Vancouver
Public Library, #39047; 26 Vancouver City
Archives; 27 University of British Columbia
Special Collections, Cumyow Family Papers;
28 Vancouver Public Library; 29 Vancouver
Public Library; 30 Provincial Archives of
British Columbia, #D-336; 31 Manitoba
Chinese Historical Society; 32 Saskatchewan
Archives Board, #5-B5095; 33 Saskatchewan
Archives Board, #R-B 7329; 35 Vancouver
Public Library; 37 Mrs. Robert Shun Wong;
38 Vancouver Public Library 42 Vancouver
Public Library; 43 University of British
Columbia Special Collections, Cumyow
Family Papers; 45 Paul Yee; 46 Vancouver
Public Library; 47 Jean Lumb; 48 Jean Lumb;
49 top Manitoba Chinese Historical Society;
bottom Ken Pearson; 50-55 Ken Pearson; 56
Vancouver Chinese Cultural Centre; 57

Calgary Chinese Cultural Centre; 63 both
pictures courtesy Ming Pao Newspapers
(Canada)Ltd; 65 Ken Pearson; 70 courtesy
Ming Pao Newspapers (Canada) Ltd.; 71 Ken
Pearson; 72 Adrienne Clarkson, Photo
Credit: Beverley Rockett; 73 A. Sung; 74 top
Keith Lock; bottom Mina Shum, First
Generation Films; 75 top Mina Shum, Photo
Credit: Kirk Tougas; bottom Sook-Yin Lee,
MuchMusic; 77 The Honourable David Lam;
78 Dr. Tak Mak; 79 top Edmonton Eskimo
Football Club; bottom Tennis Canada, Credit:
Ron Turenne; 80 top SKY Lee, Press Gang
Publishers, Photo Credit: Bon Hsiang; bot-
tom Evelyn Lau, Coach House Publishers; 81
by permission of Red Deer College Press;
Photographs of Cumyow family and Won
Alexander Cumyow reproduced by kind
permission of Victor Cumyow.

J28